COASTAL WALKS IN ANDALUCÍA

by Guy Hunter-Watts

Updated by Mike Yeatman

JUNIPER HOUSE, MURLEY MOSS,
OXENHOLME ROAD, KENDAL, CUMBRIA LA9 7RL
www.cicerone.co.uk

© Guy Hunter-Watts 2025
Second edition 2025
ISBN-13: 978 1 78631 265 5
First edition 2016
Printed in the UK by 4edge using responsibly sourced paper.
A catalogue record for this book is available from the British Library.

Route mapping by Lovell Johns www.lovelljohns.com
Contains OpenStreetMap.org data © OpenStreetMap contributors, CC-BY-SA. NASA relief data courtesy of ESRI

Cicerone's EU representative for GPSR compliance is Easy Access System Europe, Mustamäe tee 50, 10621 Tallinn, Estonia. Email gpsr.requests@easproject.com. All photographs are by the authors unless otherwise stated.

Acknowledgements

With thanks to James Stuart for help in the Vejer area, Richard Cash for his Cabo de Gata suggestions and Antonio Berruguilla Pérez from Huerta Grande for his help when I was in and around Tarifa. (Guy)

In fully updating this edition in 2024, I am always indebted to Guy for putting together a fantastic collection of walks. My thanks to Christine, my eternal walking companion, plus our trekking friends Katya Broersen and Ivo Schrijnemaekers' for their input, especially around Tarifa. (Mike)

Updates to this Guide

While every effort is made by our authors to ensure the accuracy of guidebooks as they go to print, changes can occur during the lifetime of an edition. Any updates that we know of for this guide will be on the Cicerone website (www.cicerone.co.uk/1265/updates), so please check before planning your trip. We also advise that you check information about such things as transport, accommodation and shops locally. Even rights of way can be altered over time. We are always grateful for information about any discrepancies between a guidebook and the facts on the ground, sent by email to updates@cicerone.co.uk.

Register your book: To sign up to receive free updates, special offers and GPX files where available, create a Cicerone account and register your purchase via the 'My Account' tab at www.cicerone.co.uk.

Front cover: Approaching Cala de San Pedro (Walk 40)

CONTENTS

Symbols used on route maps

route		building
alternative route		church/shrine
tunnel on route		pass
footpath		bridge
track		picnic area
vehicle track		cemetery
tarmac road		parking
(S) start point		spring
(F) finish point		water feature
(SF) start/finish point		mirador/viewpoint
> direction of route		cattle grid
woodland		wind turbines
urban areas		other feature
regional border		
lighthouse		
footbridge		
→ direction arrow		
pylon		
cave		
station/railway		
peak		
camping		

Relief
in metres

2000–2200
1800–2000
1600–1800
1400–1600
1200–1400
1000–1200
800–1000
600–800
400–600
200–400
0–200

SCALE: 1:50,000

0 kilometres 0.5 1

0 miles 0.5

Contour lines are drawn at 25m intervals and highlighted at 100m intervals.

GPX files

GPX files for all routes can be downloaded for free at www.cicerone.co.uk/1265/gpx.

5

Stone pines close to the Caños de Meca cliff path (Walk 4)

ROUTE SUMMARY TABLE

Walk no	Start	Grade	Distance	Ascent/ descent	Time	Page
Costa de la Luz						
Parque Natural de la Breña y las Marismas						
1	Santa Lucía	Medium	11km	275m	2hr 40min	39
2	nr Vejer	Easy	12.5km	15m	3hr 5min	45
3	Vejer	Medium/ difficult	18km	460m	4hr 45min	49
4	Los Caños de Meca	Medium/ difficult	18km	315m	5hr	55
5	Los Caños de Meca	Medium	14km	50m/20m	3hr 30min	60
Parques Naturales de Los Alcornocales y del Estrecho						
6	Valdevaqueros	Medium	9.5km	375m	3hr	69
7	nr Pelayo	Easy/medium	6.5km	200m	1hr 35min	74
8	Pelayo	Medium/ difficult	19km	600m	5hr	77
9	nr Algeciras	Medium/ difficult	11km	475m	3hr 20min	83
10	Gibraltar	Medium	9.5km	500m	2hr 50min	88
Costa del Sol						
Paraje Natural de Sierra Bermeja y Sierra Crestellina						
11	nr Manilva	Medium	10km	445m	3hr 5min	97
12	Casares	Medium	10km	550m	3hr 15min	102
13	Casares	Medium	10.5km	530m	3hr	107
14	nr Casares	Medium	12km	500m	3hr 15min	112
15	nr Estepona	Easy/medium	7km	350m	2hr 30min	117
La Sierra Blanca, Parque Nacional de La Sierra de Las Nieves						
16	Istán	Medium/ difficult	14km	575m	4hr 20min	124
17	Istán	Medium	14.5km	570m	4hr	128
18	Istán	Easy/medium	6km	310m	2hr	133
19	nr Marbella	Difficult	13.5km	1275m	5hr 30min	137
20	Refugio de Juanar	Medium/ difficult	15km	720m	5hr	142
21	Refugio de Juanar	Easy/medium	8km	530m	2hr 30min	146

Walk no	Start	Grade	Distance	Ascent/ descent	Time	Page
La Sierra de Mijas						
22	Mijas	Medium/ difficult	14km	850m	4hr 55min	153
23	Mijas	Medium/ difficult	11.5km	550m	3hr 15min	158
24	Alhaurín el Grande	Medium/ difficult	11.5km	740m	4hr	162
25	nr Alhaurín de la Torre	Medium	12.7km	440m	3hr 15min	167
26	Alhaurín de la Torre	Medium/ difficult	13km	570m	4hr 15min	172
27	Benalmádena	Medium/ difficult	8km	540m	2hr 50min	177
Costa Tropical						
Parque Natural de la Sierra de Tejeda, Almijara y Alhama						
28	Canillas de Aceituno	Difficult	19.5km	1675m	7hr 35min	186
29	Cómpeta	Medium/ difficult	18.5km	755m	5hr 45min	191
30	Frigiliana	Medium	8.5km	730m	3hr	197
31	Frigiliana	Medium	8.5km	510m	3hr	201
32	nr Nerja	Medium/ difficult	15km	375m	4hr 20min	205
33	Maro	Medium/ difficult	14.5km	930m/ 660m	5hr 10min	210
34	nr La Herradura	Medium/ difficult	11km	550m	3hr 30min	215
Costa de Almería						
Parque Natural de Níjar-Cabo de Gata						
35	San José	Medium	11.5km	335m	3hr 30min	224
36	Presillas Bajas	Easy	7km	275m	1hr 50min	229
37	Los Escullos	Medium/ difficult	18km	400m	5hr	232
38	Rodalquilar	Medium/ difficult	19km	575m	5hr 20min	239
39	Las Negras	Medium	16km	350m	4hr 30min	246
40	Agua Amarga	Medium	13.5km	550m	4hr 15min	251

9

Looking west towards Nerja from La Caleta (Walk 34)

PREFACE

In my mind there are two constants in Andalucía: the sea and the mountains. It is such a thrill and privilege, I believe, to be able to experience both in such a dramatic, varied fashion when walking in the coastal ranges of this beautiful country. We walk for many reasons, from simple exercise to pleasant company, but to have soaring vistas and the vastness of the ocean as companions makes every outing special.

Having walked through Andalucía following the GR7 trail from Tarifa to the state border of Murcia in 2017, I was struck by the number of mountains that weren't part of the prescribed route but invited future exploration. This desire ultimately saw us moving here to live in the Grazalema Park in 2020. Fortunately for me, Guy Hunter-Watts had made his home here much earlier and his own explorations gave rise to a number of guidebooks covering many parts of Andalucía. Inevitably, perhaps, we met and became friends. It has been simultaneously both a sad and joyous task to walk and update these walks for this, the latest edition of *Coastal Walks in Andalucía*.

The book's aim is to describe the best walking trails in seven of Andalucía's beautiful natural parks that are spread across the southern coast. The routes are located close to stunning villages and towns. Most are circular. All of the walks are within reach of anyone in reasonable health who walks on a regular basis. That said, there are routes that involve steep terrain, sometimes loose ground and occasional big drops just off the path. Always read the route description and information box so as to know what to expect.

The Subbética chain of mountains running through Andalucía is a varied, rumpled and grand set of valleys and ridges with some high peaks. This book takes you into the heart of the matter, often in wild countryside. Walkers looking for a broader spread of mountainous walks throughout Andalucía should look out for the companion guide, *Walking in Andalucía*.

If you live in this area, you won't be more than a couple of hours' drive from most trailheads and often much closer. If you're coming to Spain for a walking holiday then you can easily build a week's walking around any of the areas detailed. As a bonus, you will be close to the sea and could make a base in one of Spain's most famous and pretty towns, such as Mijas or Frigiliana.

Updating this book has been a huge journey of discovery. So many walks have been genuinely surprising in terms of scenery, grandeur and overall experience. It has been a revelation.

Mike Yeatman, 2025

The Sierra de Alhama close to Cómpeta (Walk 29)

INTRODUCTION

Looking seaward from La Maroma's 2066m summit (Walk 28)

Talk to most people about the coast of Andalucía and they'll picture the small swathe of seaboard that runs from Torremolinos to Estepona, the heartland of what is commonly sold as the Costa del Sol. First associations are of crowded beaches, busy coastal roads and blocks of holiday apartments. Few will conjure up visions of the mighty chain of mountains, the tail end of the Sierra Subbética, which rises a few kilometres back from the sea. Nor do they tend to evoke the wilder beaches of the Costa de la Luz or the footpaths that run just a few metres from the Atlantic surf.

Since Iberian times these coastal paths have seen the passage of livestock, charcoal, fruit and vegetables, dried fish, ice from the high sierras, silks and spices from distant lands, contraband coffee and tobacco, along with muleteers and shepherds, itinerant workers, fortune seekers and armies on the march. Ancient byways have a logic of their own, and while researching this book I was constantly struck by a sense of Times Past, and not only when a section of ancient paving or cobbled path suggested Roman or Arabic origins. This sense of history, and of continuity, gives nearly all of the walks described in this book an added appeal. It's as if these ancient byways serve to reconnect us with something that has been around since time immemorial but that we rarely get the chance to experience.

If the areas described in the book share a common historical thread, the different parts of the Costa have their own unique character. The cliffs, pine forests and marshlands close to Vejer are very different in feel to the wooded slopes of the Algeciras hinterland with its unique *canuto* (gorge) ecosystem. The lunaresque landscapes of the Sierra Bermeja stand in marked contrast to the forested mountainsides behind Marbella and Mijas, while the cliffs and crumpled massif of the sierras between Nerja and Almuñécar have a beauty all of their own, as do the mineral landscapes of Cabo de Gata. Each region is described in greater detail in its corresponding section, but – rest assured – there's superb walking in every one of them.

There are many terms to describe a protected area in Andalucía: UNESCO Biosphere Reserve, Parque Natural, Paraje Natural and so on. All seven coastal regions described fall into one of these categories. Waymarking on many trails is much improved since the first edition of this guide, but this only partially covers the routes described in this book, and in many cases marker posts are damaged or missing. But with the map sections and walking notes, and the GPS tracks if you use them, you'll have no problems finding your way.

The walks in this book are generally one of three types. There are

walks that link different coastal villages, others that are circular itineraries, which involve some walking at the ocean's edge, and a third group of inland circuits and gorge walks just a few kilometres back from the sea. At some point during all of the walks you'll be treated to vistas of the Atlantic or the Mediterranean.

SEVEN COASTAL REGIONS

The different walking areas are arranged in seven sections, which correspond to the different natural parks and protected areas, or combinations of these. In just a few instances the walks described fall just outside official park boundaries. At the beginning of each chapter you'll find a more detailed overview of each area. The brief description that follows will give an idea of the kind of walking and terrain you can expect to encounter. The first two natural parks are on the Costa de la Luz; the next four are on the Costa del Sol.

La Breña y las Marismas

The five walks listed are all close to the towns of Vejer, Conil, Los Caños de Meca and Zahara de los Atunes. Most walks follow footpaths very close to the ocean, apart from the Marismas circuit, a marsh walk just a few kilometres inland, and the Santa Lucía circuit, which is a 15min drive from the ocean and explores the hills north of Vejer. Gradients are generally gentle in the coastal hinterland, while

sea breezes help to make even summer walking enjoyable.

Los Alcornocales y el Estrecho

The five walks described are close to Los Barrios, Pelayo, Bolonia and Gibraltar. I've listed a Gibraltar walk in a southern Spanish walking guide because it's a stunning excursion and easy to access. Three walks follow footpaths along the ocean's edge, while the other two, which involve more climbing, introduce you to the beautiful southern flank of the Alcornocales park and its unique *canuto* ecosystem.

Sierra Bermeja y Sierra Crestellina

Of the five walks listed, two lead out from Casares, one from close to the village and another from a point just north of Manilva, while the Pico Reales circuit involves a short drive north from Estepona. Although all

walks lie a few kilometres inland, you can expect incredible views of the Mediterranean, Morocco and Gibraltar. Be prepared for sections of steepish climbing on all walks, although none are graded 'difficult'.

If you plan to undertake other walks in the region, be aware that a large swathe of the park to the east and northeast of Picos Reales was affected by a devastating forest fire in September 2021.

La Sierra de las Nieves

Of the six walks described, one leads out from Marbella and two from Refugio de Juanar, while three hikes begin in the pretty mountain village of Istán. Most walks involve steep sections of climbing, although two are quite short. The magnificent Concha ascent is one of the few walks within these pages for which a head

Casares, seen from the west (Walk 13)

for heights is required, and there are a couple of points where you'll need to use your hands as well as your feet.

La Sierra de Mijas

The six walks described begin in the villages of Mijas, Benalmádena, Alhaurín de la Torre and Alhaurín el Grande and lead you to the most beautiful corners of the compact, yet stunningly varied, landscape of the Sierra de Mijas. All walks involve sections of steep climbing, while all are easy to follow thanks to the recent restoration of waymarking of the local PR and GR footpaths.

Sierras de Tejeda, Almijara y Alhama

The villages of Cómpeta, Canillas de Aceituno and Frigiliana are all situated high on the southern flank of the Sierra de Almijara on the Costa Tropical. All three look out to the Mediterranean and their history and economy have always been inextricably linked to that of the coast. The Maroma ascent, the Imán trail and the Blanquillo circuit are big, full-day walks; the exhilarating gorge walk just inland from Nerja is not to be missed; while the La Herradura circuit leads past two of the Costa Tropical's most beautiful beaches.

Níjar-Cabo de Gata

The volcanic landscapes of the Cabo de Gata region on the Costa de Almería are unique to southern Spain, and walks here have a haunting beauty all of their own. In all but the summer months you can expect to meet with few other walkers, and the small coastal villages of Agua Amarga, Las Negras and San José have a great range of accommodation for all budgets. The best time of year to be here is spring, when the desert-like landscapes briefly take on a hue of green, while in winter this is the region of Andalucía where you're most likely to see warm and sunny weather.

PLANTS AND WILDLIFE

Two major highlights of any walk in southern Spain come in the form of the flowers and birds you see along the way.

Andalucía is among the best birding destinations in Europe and ornithological tourism has grown rapidly in recent years. The best time for birdwatching is during the spring and autumn migrations between Europe and North Africa, but at any time, in all the parks covered in this guide, you can expect rich birdlife. As well as seasonal visitors there are more than 250 species present throughout the year.

The marshes close to Barbate are one of the best sites in southern Spain for observing wading birds, both sedentary and migratory, while at the eastern end of Andalucía the

Looking north into the Higuerón gorge (Walk 30)

(clockwise from top) Griffon vulture, bee-eater and crested lark
(images courtesy of Richard Cash of Alto Aragón)

salt flats of the Cabo de Gata Natural Park provide a superb observatory for wader and duck species such as ibis, spoonbills and coots, as well as greater flamingos.

One of Europe's most remarkable wildlife events is the annual migrations across the Strait of Gibraltar. These offer the chance to observe thousands of raptors including Egyptian, griffon and black vultures; golden, imperial, booted and Bonelli's eagles; honey buzzards and harriers, as well as storks and smaller passerines. The birds circle up on the thermal currents then glide between the two continents. The migration into Spain takes place between February and May, while birds heading south can be seen from August through to late October.

For further information about birding resources and organised birding tours and walks, see Appendix A (Useful contacts).

The southern coastline also offers rich rewards for botanists. Forty per cent of all species found in Iberia are present in Andalucía and many of these grow in the coastal region. The annual wildflower explosion in late spring is as good as any in southern Europe, especially in areas where the rural exodus has ensured that much of the land has never seen the use of pesticides.

Vertebrates are less easy to spot but are also present. Along with the grazing goats, sheep, cattle and Iberian pigs, you may see squirrels, hares, rabbits, deer, wild boar, otters and mongoose. Ibex (*Capra pyrenaica hispanica*) are making a rapid comeback in many of the regions described here, especially in the Sierra de Tejeda and on the southern flank of the Sierra de Ojén. And on the Gibraltar walk you'll certainly have close encounters with Barbary apes as you follow the high ridgeline from O'Hara's Battery.

Andalucía has a long roll call of reptiles. Of its many species of snake just one is poisonous, the Lataste's viper, which is rarely seen in the coastal areas. Iberian and wall lizards are common, as are chameleons,

Wildflowers in spring

while the much larger ocellated lizard can often be seen near the coast and especially along the *ramblas* (dry river beds) of Cabo de Gata.

Appendix D (Further reading) includes details of guidebooks that will help you to identify the plants and wildlife of Andalucía.

ANDALUCÍA OVER THE YEARS

Anyone who's travelled to other parts of the Iberian Peninsula will be aware of the marked differences between the regions of Spain and their peoples. If Franco sought to impose a centralist and authoritarian system of government on his people, the New Spain, ushered in with his death and the advent of liberal democracy, actively celebrates the country's diverse, multilingual and multi faceted culture.

But if Spain is *diferente*, as the marketing campaigns of the 90s and Noughties would have us believe, then Andalucía is even more so. It is, of course, about much more than the stereotypical images of flamenco, fiestas, castanets, flounced dresses, sherry and bullfighting: any attempt to define what constitutes the Andaluz character must probe far deeper. But what very quickly becomes apparent on any visit to the region is that this is a place of ebullience, joie de vivre, easy conversation and generous gestures. The typical Andalusian's first loves are family, friends and his or her

Close encounter of the bovine kind in the Breña forest (Walk 4)

Roman ruins on the Atlantic Coast near Tarifa

patria chica (homeland), and it's rare to meet one who isn't happy to share it all with outsiders.

What goes to make such openness of character is inextricably linked to the region's history and its geographical position at the extreme south of Europe, looking east to Europe, west to the Atlantic and with just a short stretch of water separating its southernmost tip from Africa. This is a land at the crossroads between two continents, at the same time part of one of the richest spheres of trade the world has ever known: the Mediterranean Basin. Visitors from faraway places are nothing new!

A thousand years before Christ, the minerals and rich agricultural lands of Andalucía had already attracted the interest of the Phoenicians, who established trading posts in Málaga and Cádiz. But it was under the Romans, who ruled Spain from the 3rd century BC to the 5th century AD, that the region began to take on its present-day character. They established copper and silver mines, planted olives and vines, cleared land for agriculture, and built towns, roads, aqueducts, bridges, theatres and baths, while imposing their native language and customs. Incursions by Vandals and then Visigoths ended their rule, but its legacy was to be both rich and enduring.

The arrival of the Moors

If Rome laid the foundations of Andalusian society in its broadest sense, they were shallow in comparison to those that would be bequeathed in the wake of the expeditionary force that sailed across the Strait in 711 under the Moorish commander Tariq.

After the death of the Prophet, Islam had spread rapidly through the Middle East and across the north of Africa, and the time was ripe for taking it into Europe. Landing close to Gibraltar, Tariq's army decisively defeated the ruling Visigoths in their first encounter. What had been little more than a loose confederation of tribes, deprived of their ruler, offered little resistance to the advance of Islam across Spain. It was only when Charles Martel defeated the Moorish army close to the banks of the Loire in 732 that the tide began to turn and the Moors looked to consolidate their conquests rather than venture deeper into Europe.

A first great capital was established at Toledo, and it became clear that the Moors had no plans to leave in a hurry: Andalucía was to become part of an Islamic state for almost eight centuries.

Moorish Spain's Golden Age took hold in the 8th century, when Jews, Christians and Moors established a *modus vivendi* the likes of which has rarely been replicated, and which yielded one of the richest artistic periods Europe has known. Philosophers, musicians, poets, mathematicians and astronomers from all three religions helped to establish Córdoba as a centre for learning second to no other in

The cathedral of Santa Maria in Ronda, which has an Arab minaret as its bell tower

the West, at the centre of a trading network that stretched from Africa to the Middle East and through Spain to northern Europe.

However, the Moorish kingdom was always under threat, and the Reconquest – a process that was to last more than 800 years – gradually gained momentum as the Christian kingdoms of central and northern Spain became more unified. Córdoba fell in 1031, Sevilla in 1248, and the great Caliphate splintered into a number of smaller *taifa* kingdoms.

The Moors clung on for another 250 years, but the settlements along *la frontera* fell in the early 1480s, Ronda in 1485, Málaga and Vélez in 1487, and finally Granada in 1492. The whole of Spain was once again under Christian rule.

Spain's Golden Age

If ever anybody was in the right place at the right time – that's to say in the Christian camp at Santa Fe when Granada capitulated – it was the Genoese adventurer Cristóbal Colón, aka Christopher Columbus. His petition to the Catholic monarchs for funding for an expedition to sail west in order to reach the East fell on fertile soil.

The discovery of America, and along with it the fabulous riches that would make their way back to a Spain newly united under Habsburg rule, was to usher in Spain's *Siglo de Oro,* or Golden Age. Spain's Empire would soon stretch from the Caribbean through Central and South America and on to the Philippines; riches flowed back from the colonies at a time when Sevilla and Cádiz numbered among the wealthiest cities in Europe. The most obvious manifestation of this wealth, and nowhere more so than in Andalucía, was the palaces, churches, monasteries and convents that were built during this period: never again would the country see such generous patronage of the Arts.

However, by the end of the 16th century Spain's position at the centre of the world stage was under threat. A series of wars in Europe depleted Spain's credibility as well as the state coffers: by the late 17th century Spanish power was in free fall. It

remained a spent force into the 19th century, and yet further violent conflict in the early 20th century led to General Francisco Franco ('El Caudillo') sweeping into power in 1936.

Franco's crusade

Franco's 'crusade' to re-establish the traditional order in Spain – the Spanish Civil War – lasted three years, during which an estimated 500,000 Spaniards lost their lives. The eventual victory of the Nationalists in 1939 led to Franco's consolidation and centralisation of power and the establishment of an authoritarian state that remained until his death in 1975.

Franco had hoped that King Juan Carlos, who he'd appointed as his successor prior to his death, would continue to govern much in his image;

A monument to victims of the Civil War, close to Ronda

but the young king knew which way the tide was running and immediately began to facilitate the creation of a new constitution for Spain and, along with it, parliamentary democracy. Andalucía, like several other regions of Spain, saw the creation of an autonomous *Junta*, or government, based in Sevilla.

The 80s, 90s and Noughties were very good years for Andalucía, during which it saw its infrastructure rapidly transformed. New roads, schools, hospitals and hotels were built, along with a high-speed train line from Sevilla to Madrid. The huge construction boom put money into many a working person's pocket; Andalucía had never had it so good.

Tourism continues to be a major motor of the Andalusian economy, along with the construction industry, fuelled by expats setting up home in the south and other foreigners buying holiday homes and flats. The economic downturn of the last decade hit the region hard with unemployment levels reaching unpleasant, historical highs. However, since 2016 matters have improved markedly. Happily or sadly, depending on your outlook, construction works are back on the coastal strips in force. Aside from typical Costa tourism there is a large increase in so-called 'inland' tourism, where visitors come to walk in the mountains and villages described in this book. That said, you'll have many routes to yourself.

GETTING THERE

By air

For walks on the Atlantic Coast the best choice of airports are Sevilla, Jerez and Gibraltar. The latter two are also within easy range of the western Costa del Sol. Málaga is the better choice for walks close to Marbella, Mijas and the Costa Tropical. Málaga also has charter flights from all major cities in the UK, as well as scheduled flights with British airlines and Iberia. The nearest airports to Cabo de Gata, at the eastern end of Andalucía, are those at Granada, Almería and Murcia.

By car

Car hire in Spain is inexpensive when compared with that in other European destinations, and all the major companies are represented at all airports. Prices for car hire from Málaga tend to be lower. Public transport is surprisingly limited in the coastal area so hiring a car will make trip planning much easier, especially when trailheads are away from the village centres.

By train and bus

None of the seven regions described have direct access to the rail network. It is possible to travel by train to Jerez, Cádiz, Málaga or Almería and then travel on by bus or taxi to the different parks. Bus transport along the Atlantic Coast is more limited than that along the Mediterranean Coast, and even more so within Cabo de Gata.

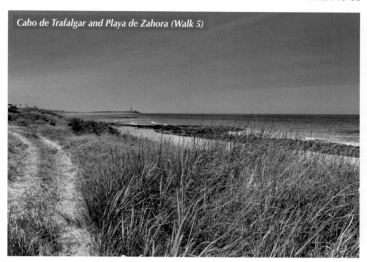
Cabo de Trafalgar and Playa de Zahora (Walk 5)

WHEN TO GO

As a general rule, the best time to walk in Andalucía is from March through to June and from September to late October. This is when you're likely to encounter mild, sunny weather: warm enough to dine *al fresco* yet not so hot as to make temperature an additional challenge. Wildflowers are at their best in late April/early May, and this is the time when many walking companies plan their walks.

Most walkers avoid July and August, when temperatures regularly reach the mid to high 30s, making walking much more of a challenge. That said, if you limit yourself to shorter circuits, get going early and take plenty of water, you can still enjoy walking in high summer.

Indeed, many of the walks here were updated in high summer.

If you're prepared to risk seeing some rain then winter is a wonderful time to be out walking, especially from December to February, when rainfall is generally less than in November, March and April. 'Generally' means exactly that: rainfall statistics for the past century confirm winter's relative dryness – although the past three decades, with three prolonged droughts followed by some unusually wet winters, provide no steady yardstick on which to base your predictions.

The most obvious choice for winter walking is Cabo de Gata: it's one of the driest areas in Europe and has

25

La Plaza de España, Vejer de la Frontera (Walk 3, Costa de la Luz)

many more hours of winter sunshine than other areas in southern Spain.

When planning excursions to the Atlantic Coast close to Tarifa it's always worth checking to see if levante winds are expected. When the wind is blowing hard through the Strait, beach walking can become a real battle against the whipped up sands.

It's always worth checking out one of the better wind websites like www.windguru.cz

ACCOMMODATION

If Andalusian tourism was once all about traditional beach and hotel tourism, the past 40 years have seen a huge growth in the numbers of visitors who come to discover its walking

trails. Villages just back from the coast tend to be the best first choice when it comes to small hotel and B&B-style accommodation, where prices are generally low in comparison to the hotels of the coastal resorts. As a rule of thumb, for €65–€85 you should be able to find a decent hotel room for two with its own bath or shower room, and breakfast will often be included.

The contact details of recommended hotels, hostels and B&Bs in and around the villages where walks begin or end are listed, by region, in Appendix B. All of the places have been visited by the authors and all are clean and welcoming. Most listings offer breakfast as well as evening meals, while some can also prepare picnics given prior warning.

Nearly every hotel, B&B and self-catering let in Andalucía is listed on www.booking.com or www.airbnb.com where, in theory, you should get the lowest price. Bear in mind, though, that by contacting the hotel directly you'll be saving them the commission they pay to these twin behemoths so they're often happy to offer a slightly lower price. However, these two websites and TripAdvisor (www.tripadvisor.co.uk) are good starting points if you wish to read about other guests' experiences at any given place.

Hotels in Andalucía make extensive use of marble. It's a perfect material for the searing heat of the summer, but in winter marble floors can be icy cold. Pack a pair of slippers: they can be a godsend if travelling when the weather is cold. And when sleeping in budget options during cold weather it's worth ringing ahead to ask the owners if they'd mind switching on the heating before your arrival. Remember, too, that cheaper hostels often don't provide soap or shampoo.

When checking in at hotel receptions expect to be asked for your passport. Once its details have been noted down, Spanish law requires that it's returned to you.

EATING OUT IN SOUTHERN SPAIN

Historically, Andalucía was not known particularly as a gourmet destination. However, much has changed in the past two decades and very good food can be found in most towns and bigger villages, corresponding, perhaps, to the influx of more discerning settlers and visitors. In smaller villages it remains true that much of the menu will come from the deep freeze, the exceptions being the cabinets filled with fresh tapas found in most bars. These can provide a delicious meal in themselves.

A tapa (taking its name from the lid or 'tapa' that once covered the jars in which they were stored) has come to mean a saucer-sized plate of any one dish, served to accompany an apéritif before lunch or dinner. If you wish to have more of any particular tapa, you can order a *ración* (a large plateful) or a *media ración* (half that amount). Two or three *raciones* shared between two, along with a mixed salad, would make a substantial and inexpensive meal.

When eating à la carte don't expect there to be much in the way of vegetables served with any meal: they just don't tend to figure in Andalusian cuisine. However, no meal in southern Spain is complete without some form of salad, which is where Andalusians get their vitamin intake. And fresh fruit is always available as a dessert.

Bear in mind that there's always a *menú del día* (set menu) available at lunchtime – even if waiters will try to push you towards eating à la carte – and many restaurants now also offer the *menú del día* in the evenings. Although you have less choice – generally two or three starters, mains and

27

desserts – the fact that set menus are often prepared on the day, using fresh rather than frozen ingredients, means this can often be the best way to eat.

Expect to pay between €8 and €15 for a three-course set menu, which normally includes a soft drink, a beer or a glass of wine. When eating à la carte, in most village restaurants you can expect to pay around €25–€35 per head for a three-course meal including beverages, while a tapas-style meal would be slightly less. Tipping after a meal is common, although no offence will be taken should you not leave a gratuity when paying smaller sums for drinks at bars.

The southern Spanish eat much later than is the custom in northern Europe. Lunch is not generally available until 2pm and restaurants rarely open before 8pm. A common lament among walkers is that breakfast is often not served at hotels until 9am, although village bars are often open from 8am. If you're keen to make an early start, pack a Thermos. Most hotels will be happy to fill it the night before, and you can always buy the makings of your own breakfast from a village shop.

Breakfasts in hotels can be disappointing, so I often head out to a local bar. Most serve far better coffee than you'll get at a hotel, freshly squeezed rather than boxed orange juice, and *una tostada con aceite y tomate* – toast served with tomato and olive

The footpath as you approach the Tajo del Caballo (Walk 24)

oil – can be a great way to start your walking day.

When shopping for the makings of your picnic, be aware that village shops are generally open from 9am to 2pm and then from 5.30pm to 8.30pm. Many smaller shops will be happy to make you up a *bocadillo* (sandwich) using the ingredients of your choice.

LANGUAGE

Visitors to Andalucía often express surprise at how little English is spoken, where even in restaurants and hotels a working knowledge of English is the exception rather than the norm. In addition, the Spanish spoken in southern Spain – Andaluz – can be difficult to understand even if you have a command of basic Spanish: it's spoken at lightning speed, with the ends of words often left unpronounced.

Appendix C offers translation of some key words that you may see on signs or maps or need to ask directions, but it's worth picking up a phrasebook before you travel – and be prepared to gesticulate: you always get there in the end. Locals can be a great help and are often delighted to engage with visitors, especially if you try at least a few words of Spanish.

MONEY

Most travellers to Spain still consider that the cost of their holiday essentials – food, travel and accommodation – is considerably lower than in northern Europe. You can still find a decent meal for two, with drinks, for around €35, and €70 should buy you a comfortable hotel room for two.

Nearly every start point village in this guide has an ATM, and where these are absent you'll generally be able to pay in shops, restaurants and hotels with a credit card. Be aware that you'll often be asked for your credit card details when booking a hotel room by phone.

COMMUNICATIONS

While most of Spain now has good mobile coverage for all major phone operators, there are still a few gaps in some of the coastal valleys – which is exactly where many of these walks will be taking you! Even so, it's always wise to have a charged phone in your daypack, preloaded with emergency contact numbers (see Appendix A, Useful contacts).

Wifi coverage is available in most hotels and is nearly always free of charge for patrons.

WHAT TO TAKE

The two most important things to take when you walk in Andalucía are:
*   water – always carry plenty of water. During the warmer months the greatest potential dangers are heat exhaustion and dehydration. Wear loose-fitting clothes and a hat, and keep drinking.

Cairn at the summit of La Concha (Walk 20)

- comfortable, broken-in walking boots – no walk is enjoyable when you've got blisters

With safety in mind, you should also carry the following:

- hat and sun block
- map and compass
- Swiss Army Knife or similar
- torch and whistle
- fully charged mobile phone (even though coverage can be patchy in the mountains)
- waterproofs, according to the season
- fleece or jumper (temperatures can drop rapidly at the top of the higher passes)
- first aid kit including antihistamine cream, plasters, bandage and plastic skin for blisters
- water-purifying tablets
- chocolate/sweets or glucose tablets
- handheld GPS device (if you have one)

This guide has been written in such a manner that all routes may be easily followed through use of the written instructions and walk maps alone; however, many hikers will wish to have a separate map too.

Under each general section I've recommended the best map available for the area; Appendix A includes the full contact details of companies from which you can buy these maps. All of the Spanish retailers will send maps *contra reembolso* (payment on receipt) to addresses within Spain.

In Andalucía the best places to order maps are LTC in Sevilla (www.ltcideas.es/index.php/mapas) and Mapas y Compañia in Málaga (www.mapasycia.es); in Madrid the best places are La Tienda Verde (www.tiendaverde.es) and Centro Nacional de Información Geográfica (www.cnig.es). In the UK the best place for maps, which can be ordered online, is Stanfords (www.stanfords.co.uk).

STAYING SAFE

When heading off on any walk, always let at least one person know where you're going and the time at which you expect to return.

Log the following emergency telephone numbers into your mobile:
- tel 112 Emergency services general number
- tel 062 Guardia Civil (police)
- tel 061 Medical emergencies
- tel 080 Fire brigade

In addition to the usual precautions, there are a few things to remember when walking in Andalucía:
- **Water** – be aware that in dry years some of the springs that are mentioned in this guide can slow to little more than a trickle or dry up altogether. Always carry plenty of water. I'd also recommend keeping a supply of water-purification tablets in your daypack.
- **Fire** – in the dry months fires are banned in almost all areas.

Wildfires are a constant threat. Wildfire Watch is a great app, giving live updates on any fires. Be very careful if you smoke. There are big fines for discarding cigarette butts.
- **Hunting areas** – signs for '*coto*' or '*coto privado de caza*' designate an area where hunting is permitted in season and not that you're entering private property. *Cotos* are normally marked with a small rectangular sign divided into a white-and-black triangle.
- **Close all gates** – you'll come across some extraordinary gate-closing devices! They can take time, patience and effort to open and close.

USING THIS GUIDE

The 40 walks in this guide are divided into seven sections, each covering a different coastal region of Andalucía. For each region there is a mixture of half-day and full-day walks that will introduce you to the most attractive areas of the particular park and lead you to its most interesting villages. The route summary table will help you select the right routes for your location, timeframe and ability.

The sections begin with a description of the area including information about its geography, plants and wildlife, climate and culture. This is followed by details of accommodation, tourist information and maps relevant to the walks described in the section.

Waymarking for the network of footpaths

The information boxes at the start of each walk provide the essential statistics: start point (and finish point if the walk is linear), total distance covered, ascent and descent, grade or rating, and estimated walking time. They also include, where relevant, notes on transport and access, and en route refreshment options (not including springs). The subsequent walk introduction gives you a feel for what any given itinerary involves.

The route description, together with the individual route map, should allow you to follow each walk without difficulty. Places and features on the map are highlighted in **bold** in the route description to aid navigation. However, you should always carry a compass and, ideally, the recommended map of the area, and a handheld GPS device is always an excellent second point of reference (see 'GPX tracks', below).

Water springs have been included in the route descriptions but bear in mind that following periods of drought they may be all but non-existent.

Rating

Walks are graded as follows:

- **Easy** – shorter walks with little height gain
- **Easy/Medium** – mid-length walks with little steep climbing
- **Medium** – mid-length walks with some steep up and downhill sections
- **Medium/Difficult** – longer routes with a number of steep up and downhill sections

If you're reasonably fit, you should experience no difficulty with any of these routes. For walks classed as Medium/Difficult, the most important things are to allow plenty of time and take a good supply of water. And remember that what can be an easy walk in cooler weather becomes a much more difficult challenge in the heat. This rating system assumes the sort of weather you're likely to encounter in winter, spring or autumn in Andalucía.

Time

These timings are based on an average walking pace, without breaks. You'll soon see if it equates roughly to your own pace, and can then adjust timings accordingly. On all routes you should allow at least an additional hour and a half if you intend to break for food, photography and rest stops.

Definition of terms

The terms used in this guide are intended to be as unambiguous as possible. In walk descriptions, 'track' denotes any thoroughfare wide enough to permit vehicle access, and 'path' is used to describe any that are wide enough only for pedestrians and animals.

You'll see references in many walks to 'GR' and 'PR'. GR stands for *Gran Recorrido* or long-distance footpath; these routes are marked with red and white waymarking. PR stands for

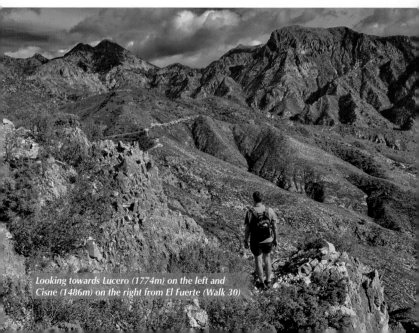

Looking towards Lucero (1774m) on the left and Cisne (1486m) on the right from El Fuerte (Walk 30)

The Gibraltar ridgeline seen from the Mediterranean Steps (Walk 10)

Pequeño Recorrido or short-distance footpath and these routes are marked with yellow and white or green and white waymarking.

GPX tracks

The GPX trail files for all of the walks featured in this guide are available as free downloads from Cicerone (www. cicerone.co.uk/1265/gpx).

By using a programme such as Garmin's BaseCamp or Komoot you can download the files to your desktop, import them into the programme and then transfer them to your handheld device. You can download Basecamp for Mac and PC at www.garmin.com/en-GB/software/basecamp.

GPX files are provided in good faith, but neither the author nor Cicerone can accept responsibility for their accuracy. Your first point of reference should always be the walking notes themselves.

The lighthouse at Cape Trafalgar (Walk 5)

1 COSTA DE LA LUZ

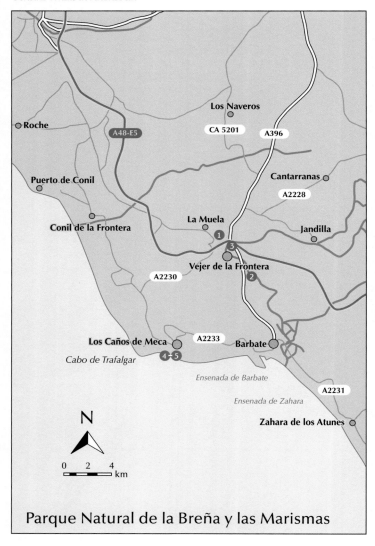

Parque Natural de la Breña y las Marismas

PARQUE NATURAL DE LA BREÑA
Y LAS MARISMAS

Track in the Barbate marshes, with Vejer in the background (Walk 2)

The Parque Natural de la Breña y las Marismas covers an area of 5077 hectares, of which one fifth fall within the marine park which stretches a kilometre out into the Atlantic. This is the smallest of Andalucía's natural parks, yet the ecosystems found within its limits are surprisingly varied, and the walks described here aim to introduce you to its three principal habitats.

Most notable is the swathe of stone pines or *pinos piñoneros* (*Pinus pinea*) of La Breña. The trees were planted in the 19th century as a means of halting the advance of the coastal dune system, which until then had little protection against the levante winds. An added bonus came in the annual harvest of nuts from the pine cones of the trees. The network of footpaths that cut through the forest

is enjoyable even in summer, thanks to the trees' dense canopies.

The ecosystem of the cliffs between Barbate and Los Caños de Meca is very different. The flora and fauna are born of the interplay of ocean spray and the sweet-water springs that rise at the base of its sand and limestone cliffs: these are the *caños* after which Los Caños de Meca was named. The cliffs rise to 100m and the path that runs along their edge (Walk 4) is a highlight of any visit to the area.

The path cuts past the Torre del Tajo, one of a string of watchtowers built in the 16th century as a deterrent to Turkish and North African corsairs who frequently raided the coastal settlements. Next to the tower are two of the finest *miradors* (viewing points) of the Andalusian seaboard: on clear days you'll see the coast of Morocco and the towering silhouette of Jebel Musa across the Strait. The cliffs are home to large colonies of gulls and are a nesting site of cattle egrets. This is one of the few places on the Atlantic Coast where you have a decent chance of spotting peregrine falcons.

The third natural jewel of the park is the wetlands of the Marismas del Río Barbate (Walk 2). The marshes are on the main migratory route to Africa and are home to a large population of resident wading birds: the dykes that criss-cross the *marismas* (marshes) are perfect ornithological viewing platforms. Stretches of the marshes were drained in the last century to create grazing for livestock but much of this land has been returned to its natural state.

The area is blessed with one of Andalucía's most exquisite towns, Vejer de la Frontera, which fans out along a ridge 7km back from the coast. The old town is an architectural arabesque, with buzzing bars and restaurants, and is home to a fast-growing expat community. Barbate is very different in feel, a modern town with dingy suburbs and one of the highest unemployment rates in Spain. The town's beach, however, is glorious, along with the adjacent coastline. There are plans to vastly improve the town's southern waterfront. The town has one of the largest fishing fleets in Spain and is best known for the annual *almadraba*, when shoals of tuna are making their way from the Atlantic to the warmer waters of the Mediterranean: the fish

are netted in much the same way as they were in Roman times. Los Caños de Meca is home to a multi-ethnic crowd of New Agers and is quiet in all but the summer months. It has a couple of excellent fish restaurants.

A further treat comes in the form of some of the finest beaches along the Costa de la Luz. To either side of the Trafalgar lighthouse, near the spot where the naval battle took place in 1805, are long stretches of fine sand where, even in summer, you can escape the crowds (Walk 5).

WHERE TO STAY

Vejer de la Frontera and Los Caños de Meca – both are close to the start points of all walks in this section – have a huge range of accommodation for all budgets. The characterful Casa del Califa in Vejer is one of Andalucía's most charming small hotels, with an excellent courtyard restaurant. See Appendix B for hotel listings.

MAPS

All five walks in the area are covered by IGN 1:50,000 Barbate 1073 (12-47).

TAXIS

Vejer de la Frontera tel 628 94 80 69
Conil de la Frontera tel 956 44 07 87 or 658 34 38 43
Los Caños de Meca (nearest taxis in Barbate) tel 623 56 43 11

WALK 1
Santa Lucía circuit

Start/finish	Iglesia Santa Lucia, Santa Lucía
Distance	11km
Ascent/descent	275m
Grade	Medium
Time	2hr 40min
Refreshments	By the A396, 100m off the route
Access	From the Cepsa petrol station just northeast of Vejer head along the N-340 towards Cádiz. Continue past the turning for Medina Sidonia then after 350m turn right at a small sign 'Santa Lucía'. Follow a narrow road for 1km to the church of Santa Lucia, which is easy to spot on the right with its towering palm tree and supporting steel structure. Park just beyond the church off to the left in the village car park. Voluntary €3 contribution towards village upkeep.

This figure-of-eight route combines two waymarked walks close to Vejer, the Route of the Watermills and the Route of the Bee-eaters. The circuit begins in the sleepy hamlet of Santa Lucía where, since Roman times, the waters of the Peñas stream have been channelled past a series of mill houses. The first section of the walk is deeply bucolic as you climb past a 16th-century aqueduct.

After a short section of tarmac road, farm tracks lead you down from La Muela then up round the southern flank of the Abejaruco peak. From here you follow ancient bridleways back to your point of departure with views south to Vejer and its rice paddies and east towards the Grazalema mountains. By setting out early you'll get back to Santa Lucía in time for lunch in one of the hamlet's three restaurants.

The walk begins outside Iglesia Santa Lucia and its huge palm tree. With your back to the church turn right up the hill past a cross and a very attractive restaurant on the left, then on reaching a water deposit, cut left up a

The Santa Lucía aqueduct near Vejer

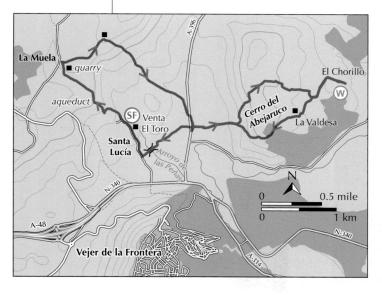

broad track which leads to a junction and a sign 'Ruta de los Molinos'. Here, cut right up a narrow path which leads up the right side of an **aqueduct** to reach an old mill fronted by a post-and-rail fence.

Pass to the right of the building, angle right beneath a cast iron pipe, then continue up a narrow, leafy path which climbs to a scruffy, more level area. From here, head straight on along a quiet minor road towards **La Muela**. After 450m you reach a fork. Here, branch right, away from the tarmac, along a sandy track which arcs round the boundary fence of a **quarry**.

Pass the quarry entrance and continue along the track past some buildings on your left to reach a T-junction with a broad track. Here, turn right and climb in an easterly direction before dipping down then once again climbing again. ▶ You will shortly reach a junction next to a house on the left with white walls and a big gate. (**30min**)

Views open out towards the mountains of the Grazalema park.

Here, turn right along a track which descends across farmland in a southeasterly direction. Vejer comes into view. Bearing right, the track runs parallel to the **A396**, passing a signboard about drovers' paths like the one you're following: Los Caminos Históricos y las

Farm track leading east from La Muela

100m along the road to your left, along the main road, is a restaurant and bar, Venta La Gitana.

Cañadas. ◀ Some 250m beyond the sign the track angles left to meet the A396. Cross the road and turn right. After 75m angle through a gap in the crash barrier and continue on along a dirt track.

Just past a villa marked Muñoz de Begines cut left along a track which soon crosses a stream via a concrete bridge then reaches a fork. Take the left branch. The track runs gently up towards the **Cerro del Abejaruco** (named after the bee-eaters that nest here) where, reaching a fork, you should bear left. Arcing left and climbing steeply you adopt a northerly course, and the track climbs to reach another junction (**1hr 10min**).

> **Bee-eaters** (*Merops apiaster*) are annual visitors to Spain, where they come to breed after wintering in tropical Africa, India and Sri Lanka. They will eat any flying insect, although their choice food is the honey bee: they can eat up to 250 in a day. The bee's stinger and poison are removed by repeatedly hitting and scraping the insects on a hard surface. Bee-eaters nest in sandy banks as part of large colonies. They number among Europe's most colourful birds and have an unusually liquid, burry song.

Here, cut right through a man-made breach in the hillside, ignoring a smaller path off to the right. The track now descends before rising again to another junction. Bearing slightly right along the main track, you reach a third junction next to a pylon with a yellow warning triangle 'Alta Tensión'. Here keep straight ahead.

The track soon descends and loops downhill, passing beneath electricity lines, to reach a junction (1hr 25min). Here, turning left along a narrow track, after some 500m you reach a junction. Turning right past a low, white building, after 150m you will see a Roman oven on the left and a damaged marker post. Here, angle hard right and follow a narrow track down through dense vegetation to reach the spring of **El Chorrillo** (**1hr 40min**). From here retrace your steps back to the junction (**2hr**).

Agave-lined track leading to the spring at El Chorrillo

On reaching the junction, head straight ahead and descend through a thick stand of bamboo then cross a (dry) stream. ▶ Beyond the stream the track climbs steeply past a modern house, where it angles right, left, then right again as it passes the house's entrance gates, marked **La Valdesa**. Crossing a ridge, Vejer again comes into view. Merging with another track and angling gently right, you shortly pass beneath another house with a sign 'Propiedad Privada'. After steeply descending an ancient, cobbled track you reach the track you followed earlier in the walk (**2hr 30min**).

From here retrace your steps back to the A396. Follow the crash barrier left for 50m then angle back right for 30m then cross the road. Reaching a large brown gate topped with spikes and flanked by grey stone and red brick posts, cut left along a track across open countryside. Descending, then angling left then right, you reach the first buildings of **Santa Lucía**. On crossing a **bridge** over the Arroyo de las Peñas, the track meets the road you followed earlier up to the village. Turn right and climb back to your point of departure (**2hr 40min**).

70m further down the road towards the coast is a restaurant on the left, Venta El Rayo, with outstanding menu del dia from €10 (in 2024).

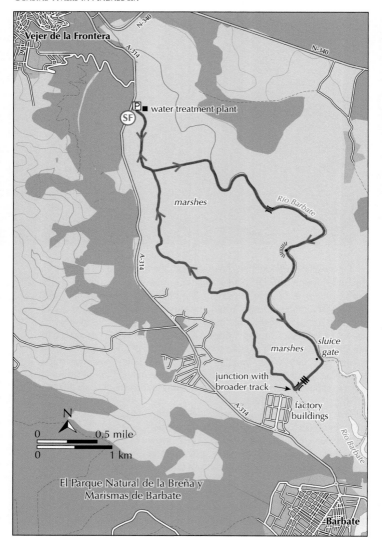

WALK 2

Las Marismas de Barbate circuit

Start/finish	Car parking area beside the A314 next to a water treatment works, near Vejer de la Frontera
Distance	12.5km
Ascent/descent	15m
Grade	Easy
Time	3hr 5min
Refreshments	None
Access	From the N-340 at La Barca, just to the east of Vejer, take the A314 towards Barbate for approximately 3km until you reach a sign 'Sendero Marismas de Barbate'. Cut left into a parking area, where the walk begins.

Since 1994 the flat delta at the mouth of the Río Barbate, Las Marismas de Barbate, has formed part of the Natural Park of La Breña. These low-lying marshlands, criss-crossed by water canals, streams and raised tracks, have a bewitching beauty and are home to richly diverse flora and fauna.

This is one of the best places on the Atlantic Coast for birding: the marshes lie on one of the major migratory routes between northern and central Europe and Africa and are used by birds as a halfway house before and after the journey across the Strait. The birds, both sedentary and migratory, feed on the abundant molluscs and crustaceans of the tidal reedbeds, and it's easy to spot egrets, mallards, grebes and herons, as well as several different warblers, among the reeds and tamarisk.

The walk is particularly memorable early on an autumn day, when the low-lying flora of the Marismas is taking on its autumnal colours and Vejer hovers above the early morning mist. Be aware that parts of the walk on the latter section of the route can be waterlogged after rain.

The walk begins in the car parking area between Las Marismas de Barbate and the A314. There is a **water treatment plant** to one side with informational sign-boards illustrating the treatment process. From the car

The Río Barbate beneath Vejer de la Frontera

From here there are fine views back across the floodplain to Vejer.

park go through a small black gate to one side of a larger, green one. Bearing right and adopting a southerly course, you'll immediately begin to spot all kinds of wading birds out in the **marshes**.

Reaching a fork next to a sign 'Parque Natural', turn left along a track which cuts due east across the marshes for a little over 700m then, just before it reaches the **Río Barbate**, angles right and runs on close to the looping course of the river. ◄

The track, bearing right, passes a newly built bridge (2023) across the river to your left. The bridge is not part of the route but does make for an excellent stop to view the marshes and birdlife from a higher vantage point. Continuing along the track away from the new bridge, the route swings back left, following the river. Here there is a **viewing platform** with an information sign listing the most commonly seen birds in the reserve. A bit further on you will find a bird hide, built in 2023. Here there is a fork. Continue straight ahead (unless you wish to shorten the walk – in which case turn right), sticking close to the bank of the Río Barbate before reaching a fork just beyond a **sluice gate**, which is to your right. Here cut right and head back to the western edge of the marshes and a group of **factory buildings**.

Crossing a small concrete bridge and reaching a sign showing a map of the reserve then a small brick bridge (**1hr 55min**), you reach a junction with a broader track. Turn right and head on towards Vejer. Passing beneath power lines the track arcs left then passes through an enclosure with a group of ramshackle animal pens. Angling right through a grove of Eucalyptus trees you reach a fork. The left fork has a concrete parapet. Take the right fork. Soon you leave the trees behind, reaching more open countryside.

The *marisma*'s rich **flora and fauna** are born of the interplay of salt water from the Atlantic with that of the Río Barbate's flood plain. Spoonbills, night heron and osprey are common sightings, along with egrets, kestrels and peregrine falcons. The marshes are also home to a huge variety of wading birds including avocet, black-winged stilt, ringed and Kentish plovers, dunlin and greater flamingos. The birds find rich pickings in the form of wedge clams, cockles and, closer to the ocean, mussels

Spanish turtle (Mauremys leprosa) in the reed beds

and prawns. Fish species inhabiting the marsh's saline waters include sole, eel, mullet, bass and gilthead bream.

The track narrows as it runs on between beds of reeds, still heading towards Vejer. There are many nesting birds in this area. At this point the track can be water-logged, leaving you with the choice of wading/paddling or retracing your steps to the left fork with the concrete parapet and making a return detour along residential tracks and the road to the start point (will add 2km.) Soon the track arcs hard right (**2hr 30min**) then left once more. Adopting its former course, it passes through thicker undergrowth where there are stands of bamboo and mimosa. Crossing a cattle grid the track runs on to reach the junction where, earlier in the walk, you cut across to the eastern side of the marsh. From here retrace your steps back to the **car park** (**3hr 5min**).

WALK 3

Vejer de la Frontera southern circuit

Start/finish	The Plaza de España at the heart of the old town of Vejer
Distance	18km
Ascent/descent	460m
Grade	Medium/Difficult
Time	4hr 45min
Refreshments	Hotel El Palomar de la Breña and Venta Los Olivos

This longish figure-of-eight walk introduces you to the rolling farmland between Vejer and the Breña Natural Park. After winding through the beautiful old town you cut along a high ridge past a number of wind turbines. How much you enjoy this part may depend on where you stand in the debate. You next follow tracks through open fields then along a hedgerow-lined drovers' path to reach a small rural hotel and El Palomar de la Breña.

A visit to (what claims to be) the world's largest dovecote is an absolute must and you'll be given a friendly welcome in the bar/cafeteria. From here sandy tracks lead to the edge of the Breña forest and the hamlet of San Ambrosio, from where you cut north back towards Vejer. Reaching the ridge with the wind turbines you could shorten the walk by retracing your steps back to Vejer. But the loop out to the west – which involves a little more climbing – is well worth the extra effort.

The walk lends itself to alternative start points and could easily be split into two shorter half-day circular routes (a preferred hot-weather alternative). A good alternative start point would be the Venta Los Olivos, whereby you could have an excellent lunch at the end of the walk plus do the main climb at the beginning of the day rather than the end. Another good start point would be the Hotel Palomar de la Breña, especially if staying on the coast.

The walk begins next to a fountain in front of the El Jardin del Califa restaurant in the Plaza de España at the eastern side of Vejer de la Frontera. With your back to the hotel pass to the left of a kiosk, angle right and pass beneath an arch. Climbing past the Vera Cruz restaurant the street angles right then left then reaches a sign 'Arco de la Segur'. Cut right and continue parallel to a line of battlements.

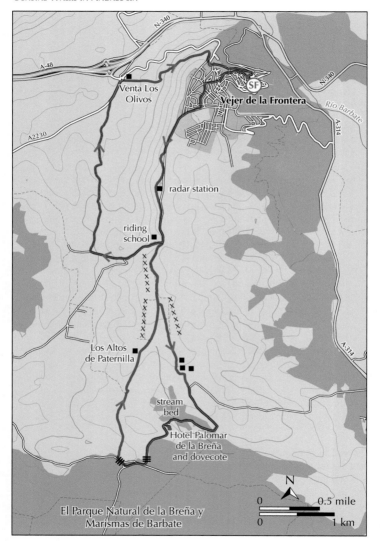

Wind turbines on the Cerro del Búho

Passing beneath the arch of Puerta de la Segur, drop down Calle Marqués de Tamarón, which soon becomes Nuestra Señora de la Oliva, to reach the Plazuela square. Here angle left along Calle Juan Relinque, following a sign Teatro San Francisco. Reaching house number 22A, cut right up Calle San Ambrosio to a stop sign then turn left along the palm-lined Avenida de Andalucía. At the end of the street, at a supermarket, cut right and climb past new urbanisations on your left. Leaving the last of the town's houses behind you, continue on a straight road heading towards the sea, with 50kmh and 'No overtaking' signs.

From here head along a sandy footpath, just right of the tarmac road, which runs towards a line of wind turbines atop a ridge. Reaching a fork, angle left back towards the road then right once more through low-growing shrubs. You shortly pass to the right of a **radar station** used by civil aviation. Views open out towards Conil and Zahara de los Atunes. Passing a picnic area the path meets with the road once more.

Continuing for 300m you reach a junction by a group of buildings. Ignoring the track that cuts down to the right, continue for 10m to a second junction then angle right past a blue and white sign 'Consorcio de Aguas de la Zona Gaditana'. The track climbs then passes the first of a line of **wind turbines**. Heading on past several

The world's largest dovecote, El Palomar de la Breña

The wire-and-post gate is very easy to miss. If you do miss it, simply climb over the metal farm gate that is just beyond it.

turbines, you reach an informational signboard on the left for El Bosque y Matorral Mediterráneo (**1hr**).

Here cut left along a narrow track which after 30m arcs right and runs on parallel to a second line of turbines. Just beyond the last turbine the track reaches a wire-and-post gate. ◄ Go through the gate then, angling right, continue towards the sea. After some 350m you reach a **group of houses** and outbuildings. Angle left along the main track, leaving the buildings to the right.

Leaving the buildings behind, continue along the track. The Hotel Palomar de la Breña comes into view on the right. At a junction take the right-hand fork. The track hugs the edge of a huge field then after some 650m loops hard right, now descending between thick hedgerows. Sandier and more eroded, the track narrows to become a path that shortly crosses a (dry) **stream bed**. Beyond the stream, after climbing steeply, you reach a track and a sign 'El Palomar de la Breña' (**1hr 45min**).

The **dovecote** (*palomar*) that gives its name to the hotel was built in the 18th century and contains 7700 niches, making it the largest in the world. The breeding birds once produced between 10 and 15 tonnes of guano or 'black gold' per year, which was used to manufacture gunpowder. Additional income was obtained through the sale of the pigeons to the aristocratic families of Cádiz at a time when pigeon was a delicacy only the wealthy could afford. The birds were also caged and taken on board ships bound for the Americas, ensuring a supply of fresh meat even when far from port. There's no entrance fee to visit the dovecote but rather a voluntary donation.

From El Palomar de la Breña continue along a broad, sandy track which leads to the edge of the forest of the Parque Natural de la Breña. Crossing a **cattle grid** the track arcs right then merges with a broader track which, running on in a westerly direction, reaches a junction with a tarmac road and a finger sign for horse riding routes to Barbate and Vejer. After turning right and crossing another **cattle grid**, you reach another junction. Here turn left then after 125m cut right at a second horse-riding sign for Vejer de la Frontera along a broad track which climbs back towards Vejer.

After leaving the last village houses you reach a fork. Here, angling right, continue along a narrower track that runs a few metres to the right of the one you've just left. After running back towards the broader track it angles right once more before meeting it once again opposite the gates of **Los Altos de Paternilla**. Continue along the main track which soon passes between the two lines of **wind turbines** before you reach the sign you passed earlier in the walk for El Bosque y Matorral Mediterráneo (**2hr 50min**). From here retrace your steps back past the last of the wind turbines to reach a group of buildings and a stop sign. ▶

From here you could shorten the walk by returning to Vejer via the same route you followed earlier in the day.

At the stop sign angle hard left down a broad track. Views open out towards the Atlantic and Conil as you descend past a **riding school** then a set of gates marked 'Buena Vista'. The track, now with a concreted surface, arcs right then hard back to the left towards a 20km speed-limit sign. Here cut right, away from the tarmac, down a dirt track. On reaching a brown wooden gate, follow the

track as it angles right then climbs past an ochre-coloured house, then reach a fork with Senderos signs for the Rutas Molinos de Vento and the Ruta Buenvista. Here keep left. After descending and angling right, the track loops left once more and resumes its former course as it cuts through a thick stand of bamboo.

On reaching the road that leads from Vejer to Los Caños de Meca, the A2230, angle right and follow the road for 350m, passing a new hospital, to reach the roundabout next to **Venta Los Olivos**. ◄ Here, bearing right and passing just right of the restaurant, cross a cattle grid and continue up a farm track that climbs steeply towards Vejer. Angling left past a No entry sign the track becomes cobbled before it narrows, now more overgrown, then crosses a wooden footbridge.

Venta Los Olivos is an excellent alternative start/finish point for the walk.

On reaching a restored windmill, the path levels then angles right to reach the first houses of Vejer where, following a tarmac road, you descend to a junction. Here bear right past a stone arch then go left at the roundabout, following the road as it goes in the direction of a sign marking Centro Ciudad, Zona Monumental. Passing a line of restaurants, continue along Calle Corredera then cut right to return to the Plaza de España (**4hr 45min**).

WALK 4
Los Caños de Meca circuit

Start/finish	Outside Hotel Madreselva in Los Caños de Meca
Distance	18km
Ascent/descent	315m
Grade	Medium/Difficult
Time	5hr
Refreshments	None en route

This longish circuit gives you the chance to sample the twin natural habitats that make the Parque Natural de la Breña such a special treat, introducing you to its vast forest of stone pines as well as to the spectacular cliffs which rise 100m above one of the best beaches in Andalucía. The walk begins with a section of forest walking as you follow sandy paths and tracks towards San Ambrosio. Here you can make a detour up to the Torre del Tajo.

After heading on towards Barbate via a broad forestry track you cut south through the stone pines to reach the A2233. Here you have a choice between following a sandy gully to reach the beginning of the cliff path that leads up to the Torre del Tajo – this adds an extra kilometre or so to the walk – or cutting straight through the forest to the Torre.

The walk is graded Medium/Difficult, not so much for the distance covered but rather because of the additional effort required when walking on the sandy paths that cut through the Breña forest.

The walk begins in Los Caños de Meca outside Hotel Madreselva, which you pass as you head east through the village on the A2233. From here head east past a row of palm trees. On reaching a green sign for the McDonalds in Barbate, turn left. The road soon arcs left. Just beyond the 'km14' sign cut left along a sandy track. After running west the road arcs right as it passes beneath the **Torre de Meca**. Reaching a three-way junction, bear right at a 'No entry' sign plus another prohibiting motorcycles and quad bikes, passing between two rusting metal posts. The track climbs gently as it runs eastwards: views open out

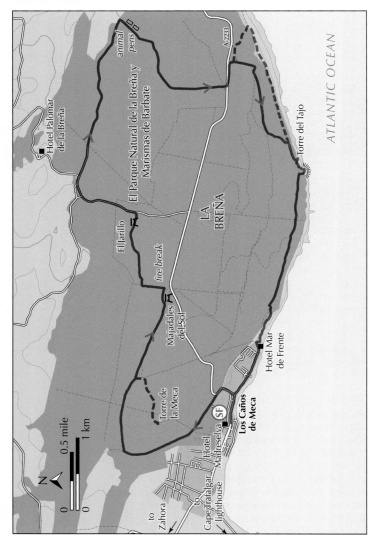

above the treetops. Shortly beyond the top of the rise you pass the path up to the Torre de Meca (**45min**).

To climb up and down to the tower, on a trail way-marked with wooden posts with white arrows, add 40 minutes to these timings and 2km to the distance.

Just beyond a sign you reach a fork. Heading straight ahead the track passes several different species of eucalyptus tree: about a dozen are marked with their Latin names. Some 35m before reaching a metal gate and the **Majadales del Sol picnic area**, cut left along a sandy track. Continue parallel to the enclosure fence then, reaching a **fire break**, cut left. Follow the fire break north for 300m then angle right along a narrow path that shortly passes a signboard about Pinares Costeras (**1hr 30min**) then reaches the edge of the **El Jarillo picnic area**. The path braids a lot on the way to El Jarillo, with multiple tracks in all directions mainly made by mountain bikers and horse riders. In general, keep to the main pathways and head in an easterly direction, maintaining a broadly straight course. If you miss the picnic area, you will hit the tarmac road that leads to it and can walk along this to find it.

After passing stone tables and benches, towards a recycling bin, you reach a tarmac road. Cutting left along the road you cross a cattle grid then after some 650m reach a junction where a sign points left for San Ambrosio. Ignoring the sign, carry on along the track which arcs right, passes a sign prohibiting access to lorries, then reaches a fork (**1hr 50min**).

Keep right along the main track (ignoring a sign left for Palomar de la Breña), which you'll now follow without forking off for a little over 2km. At first you follow a line of pylons but these soon angle away to the left. Reaching a junction by an information board marked El Pinar de Pinos Piñoneros (**2hr 20min**), turn right, away from the main track. Passing a line of **animal pens**, the track runs on through the pines before crossing a cattle grid then reaching the **A2233**.

Stone pines (*Pinus pinea*) have been cultivated for their edible pine nuts for at least 6000 years and

Stone pine forest (Pinus Pinea) in La Breña

have been used extensively as ornamental trees in gardens and parks since their popularisation at the time of the Italian Renaissance. The trees of La Breña were planted in the 19th century as a means of fixing the coastal dune system, which suffered constant transformation due to the fierce levante winds.

If you wish to walk a longer section of the cliff path turn left and continue parallel to the A2233.

Cross the road and turn left along the newly built green-surfaced cycle path next to the road. After 300m the track angles hard right. After 50m you reach a junction. To shorten the walk by 1km head straight ahead for 70m then angle right along a broad path. Follow marker posts through the forest past two signboards marked Nos Miran and Aromas del Bosque to the Torre del Tajo. ◀

Just as the track angles back towards the road you reach a cattle grid. Here angle 45 degrees to the right then after 75m cut right through the scrub and drop down to the sandy bed of a gully. Here cut left and follow a narrow, sandy path down towards the sea. The gully widens before reaching the Barbate–Caños cliff path (3hr 5min).

The path leads past a sign about Pinares Costeras or the coastal pine forest: it was planted to stabilise the dune system.

From here head west past a steep cliff face, parallel to the sea. Soon a rail-and-post barrier runs between you and the ocean. ◀ 200m past the sign you reach the **Torre del**

Tajo. Be sure to visit the **mirador** some 100m west of the tower for the finest cliff views of the walk.

> The **Torre del Tajo** is one of dozens of coastal watchtowers that were built at the end of the 16th century during the reign of Philip II to protect the southern coastline of Spain from raids by Barbary pirates.

Continuing towards Caños along the main cliff path you reach a point where the pole fence that has been to your left comes to an end. Turn right, away from the sea, to a junction. Here turn left. The sandy path now follows the long-distance path, GR145 Sendero Europeo Arco Atlántico, with its red, green and white banded marker posts, all the way back to Caños. As you descend, the Trafalgar lighthouse comes into view. On the approach to Caños there are opportunities to drop off the way-marked trail and drop down to a number of beautiful beaches and coves for a picnic or a swim. Some of the beaches may be described as 'clothing optional'. The waymarked trail continues in to Caños, passing behind the Hotel Mar de Frente. Continue along the road to the start point of the walk. (**5hr**).

The descent to the Hotel Mar de Frente

WALK 5

Cape Trafalgar to Conil via the Torre de Castilnovo

Start	Hostal Mini Golf at the western edge of Los Caños de Meca
Finish	Plaza de España in Conil de la Frontera
Distance	14km
Ascent	50m
Descent	20m
Grade	Medium
Time	3hr 30min
Refreshments	None en route. There is a bar at the finish in Conil.
Access	From Vejer take the CA2233 towards Los Caños de Meca. Approximately 1km before reaching the village, park on the left side of the road next to Hostal Mini Golf.

This linear walk takes in one of the finest sweeps of sand in southern Spain as you pass from Trafalgar to Conil via the beaches of Zahora, El Palmar and Castilnovo. From the walk's start point just west of Los Caños de Meca you follow a road, blocked to vehicles, out to the Trafalgar lighthouse before dropping down to the Atlantic, which you'll be following most of the way to Conil.

This is a great walk for birdlife with plenty of ornithological action at the ocean's edge and in the marshes you cross on the approach to Conil. Take a wind check before setting out: a strong levante whips sand hard across the beaches and can turn the walk into an ordeal rather than a pleasure.

If you set out early you could end the walk with lunch in Conil: Bar Rincón de la Villa in the corner of Plaza de España is a perfect spot for an *al fresco* meal. If you prefer a shorter walk, you could break off in El Palmar, which has several beachside bars and restaurants, or simply walk part of the way then return by the same route.

The walk begins outside **Hostal Mini Golf**. Cross the road and head towards the lighthouse following a sign 'Faro de Trafalgar'. Pass a line of bars and restaurants then a red and white barrier blocking vehicle access. Approaching the **lighthouse** along a tarmac road piled high with drifts of wind-blown sand, head across a roundabout where a plaque commemorates the 1805 naval battle.

> The **Battle of Trafalgar**, which took place just west of Cape Trafalgar, was the most decisive naval battle of the Napoleonic Wars, when the British defeated the combined fleets of France and Spain. Some 27 British ships of the line engaged 33 enemy ships. Nelson's strategy of attacking in two lines perpendicular to the enemy line marked a new beginning in naval warfare.

map continues on page 62

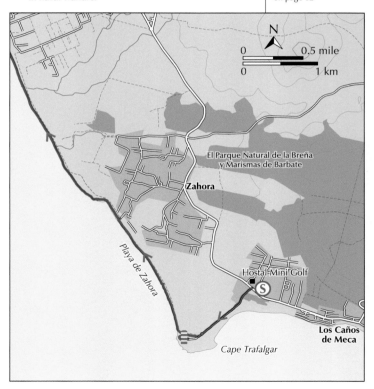

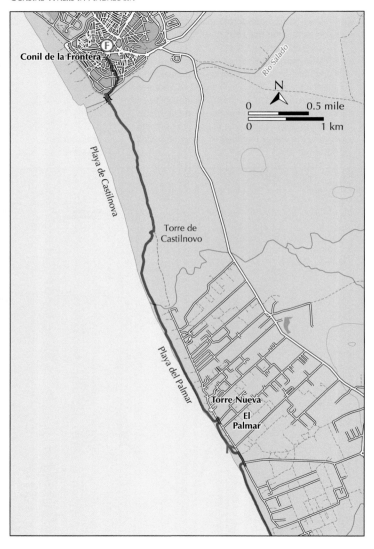

After ascending slightly and arcing right towards the lighthouse gates, cut right along a wooden walkway which descends to the beach. There is a second walkway that passes around the lighthouse to a dead end with a dramatic viewpoint. Worth the 40m detour. Having descended the walkway to its end you will find GR145 signage that warns that the route is now unmarked for the next 8.6km. Turn right along the **Playa de Zahora**, where the firmer sand at the ocean's edge makes for easier walking. At the far end of the beach, making your way across rocks just beneath an odd building on a headland with what appears to be upturned boat hulls serving as a roof (**45min**). Shortly after this you reach the start of the long **Playa del Palmar**.

Follow the path, which runs just above the beach at the edge of the dunes until it drops back to the beach, and then return to the firmer sand at the ocean's edge. The white tower of Torre Nueva, between El Palmar and the sea, comes into view.

Passing left of **Torre Nueva (1hr 50min)**, after some 750m you reach the **Playa de Castilnovo**: there's no clear demarcation between the two beaches. A square tower,

The lighthouse at Cape Trafalgar

Torre de Castilnovo

Torre de Castilnovo, is soon visible to the right of the beach. Look for a wooden-post archway to the right, nestled in the low dunes. This is the start of a boardwalk that you take towards the tower. At the archway is the mirror sign of the one you saw 8.6km back as you left Trafalgar. Follow the boardwalk to a decent track that cuts left directly to the tower. There are signboards with the history of the building. ◀

The tower is a nesting site for dozens of noisy black winged stilts.

The **almadraba** or annual blue-fin tuna catch has taken place since Phoenician times along Spain's Atlantic Coast. An elaborate labyrinth of circular nets is laid in the path of the migrating tuna, which are on the move between the Atlantic and the warmer waters of the Mediterranean. Eighty per cent of the catch is exported to Japan for making sushi and sashami.

This is a great place for ornithology: you'll almost certainly see marsh harriers hunting above the flats.

From the tower head on across the marshes via a sandy track which runs straight towards Conil, parallel to the beach. ◀ As the track reaches a concrete trig point

Playa del Palmar

marked DPMT you reach a fork. Bear left and continue with a fence now just to your right. Passing the buildings of Cortijo del Prado, which are over to your right, cross a **footbridge** over the Río Salado.

Beyond the bridge cut right, parallel to the northwest bank of the river. On reaching a damaged signboard, cut left across the street and, passing a small *kiosko* and a football pitch, head straight past a 'No entry' sign up Calle Azorín. At the top of the street bear left then take the next right in front of the Moorish-looking door of house number 8. At the next junction turn left along Calle San José then take the next right to reach Plaza de Andalucía. Here, bearing left then right, you reach Plaza de España next to Bar Rincón de la Villa at the heart of the old town of **Conil de la Frontera (3hr 30min)**.

From Plaza de España head up the hill, pass beneath an arch, then turn right to reach the taxi rank. The fare back from Conil to the walk's start point is less than €20. Or there is a daily bus departing from Conil for Caños at 18.35.

View from the bridge over the Río Salado, Playa de Castilnovo

Statue in Conil at the end of the walk

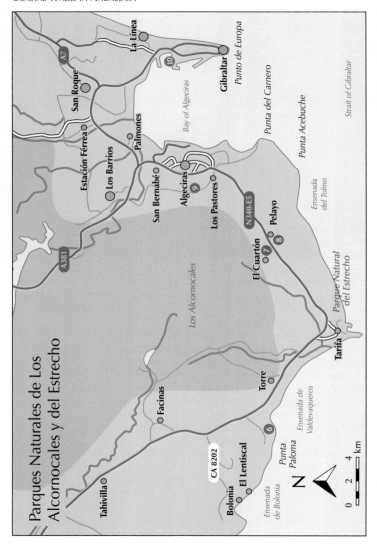

Parques Naturales de Los
Alcornocales y del Estrecho

PARQUES NATURALES DE LOS ALCORNOCALES Y DEL ESTRECHO

The home stretch to Playa de Valdevaqueros (Walk 6)

The Parque Natural del Estrecho is one of the most recently created protected areas in southern Spain. Fanning out to both sides of Tarifa as far as Bolonia to the west and Algeciras to the east, it encompasses a 19,000-hectare slice of Andalucía's Mediterranean and Atlantic coasts. This is the southernmost tip of western Europe, where just 10.5km separate the continent from Africa: on a clear day, on any walk in the area, you'll be rewarded with the sight of the Moroccan Rif rising above the Strait, while yachts, tankers and ferries plough the waters between the two coastlines.

The main protagonist here is the levante wind, which blows hard from the east for much of the year. Funnelled down as it passes through the Strait, the wind's cutting edge has been responsible for the creation of high dune systems: these rise to over 30 metres in height at the end of Bolonia's beautiful arc of sand. The region is host to one of the most extraordinary natural events of the Andalusian year: the spring and autumn migration between Europe and Africa. It's been estimated that a mind-boggling 30 million birds cross the Strait during the autumn passage, and the sight of the migration is one never to be forgotten.

The comparative lack of development along the Costa de la Luz, thanks in part to the military bases that have long existed along Spain's southern border, make this coastal strip very different in feel to parts of the Costa del Sol, while the creation of the Natural Park has effectively put an end to developers' dreams of creating more coastal resorts.

The walks described in this section to either side of Tarifa (Walks 6 and 8) lead past hidden coves and long sandy beaches, which feel a world away from the crowded ones that are just a few dozen kilometres to the east. You will, however, see a lot of action out on the waves: the kite-surfing community has made Tarifa its adopted home, and for much of the year you'll be treated to an amazing display of acrobatics off the beach at Valdevaqueros, where international competitions sometimes take place.

Two walks described in this section lie within the Parque Natural de Los Alcornocales, which runs up to the northern boundary of the Parque del Estrecho. This fringe of the park is home to one of its most beautiful tracts of cork-oak forest and to lush *laurisilva* (laurel forest) in its *canutos*, an ecosystem unique to this part of Andalucía, born of the warm and humid conditions present in the park's southernmost gullies. The Río de Guadelmesí circuit (Walk 7) cuts through this wonderful swathe of woodland, as does the Río de la Miel circuit (Walk 9), which has the added attraction of leading you past a series of idyllic rock pools.

A circular walk on Gibraltar is also included (Walk 10). Even if the Rock is not politically a part of Andalucía, it's very much present on most of these walks, rising lion-like in the distance above the Bay of Algeciras. The circuit described, which leads up Mediterranean Steps then along its knife-like ridge, is a thrilling half-day excursion and should not be missed, provided that you have a reasonable head for heights.

WHERE TO STAY

Most visitors to the area tend to gravitate towards the hotels of the old town of Tarifa or those close to the beach of Los Lances, where you'll find accommodation for all budgets. Bolonia also has a number of cheap-and-cheerful hostels and the added attraction of the exquisite Roman site of Baelo Claudia, with a state-of-the-art museum about the Roman settlement. For hotel listings see Appendix B.

MAPS

Walks 6 and 7 are covered by IGN 1:50,000 Tarifa 1077 (13–48), Walks 8 and 9 are covered by Tarifa 1077 (13–48) and Algeciras 1078 (14–48), and Walk 10 by Algeciras 1078 (14–48).

TAXIS

Bolonia/Tarifa tel 956 43 92 33
Pelayo tel 956 60 60 60
Los Barrios tel 956 62 18 72

WALK 6

Valdevaqueros circuit via Punta Paloma

Start/finish	Dunas luxury beach resort, Playa de Valdevaqueros
Distance	9.5km
Ascent/descent	375m
Grade	Medium
Time	3hr
Refreshments	None en route
Access	From Tarifa take the N-340 towards Cádiz. On reaching km post 74, exit for Punta Paloma along the A2325. Pass Camping Paloma then turn left at a sign for Playa de Valdevaqueros. Continue for 300m to the parking area just beyond Dunas luxury beach resort. The parking is free but sometimes a voluntary donation (€1.50 in 2024) may be requested.

This averagely strenuous but stunning half-day walk begins next to the beautiful sweep of sand of the Valdevaqueros beach where, on most days of the year, you'll see hundreds of kite surfers cutting their way through the waves. After passing the Bronze Age burial site of Los Algarbes a steep path leads up to the hamlet of Betijuelo from where you climb at a more gentle gradient through pine forest to a rocky promontory and the highest point of the walk.

A stunning 360-degree panorama provides a fitting reward for the climb from Los Algarbes: on a clear day you'll see the bays of Bolonia and Valdevaqueros and the Moroccan coast, as well as the jagged ridges of the southern fringe of the Alcornocales park. Cutting steeply down to the beach at Punta Paloma, you follow the ocean's edge back to your point of departure, passing two of the Atlantic Coast's most beautiful beaches.

The walk begins at a signboard 'Chorlitejo Patinegro' in the southwest corner of the car park just beyond the **Dunas luxury beach resort**, just behind the Playa de Valdevaqueros. ▸ Head back along the road past Camping El Jardín de las Dunas. On reaching the A2325 and some municipal bins on the right, head straight across the road

The board has information about the rare Kentish plovers that nest in the area.

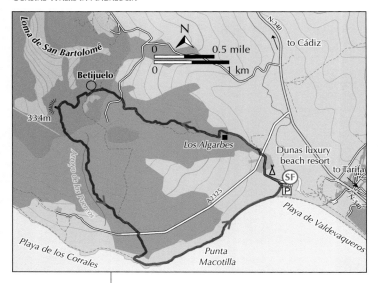

and head up a dirt track with numerous signs, including one for Rutas a Caballo, Tarifa. Shortly you pass a couple of post boxes on the left and a small stone and metal monument to Lothar Bergmann on the right.

> **Lothar Bergmann** was a German-born explorer and archaeologist who discovered more than 60 prehistoric sites, many with early cave paintings, in the province of Cádiz. He lived close to the archaeological site of Los Algarbes, where his ashes were scattered after his death in 2009.

After passing beneath a riding centre the track passes the entrance to the Bronze Age burial site of **Los Algarbes** then reaches a signboard about the route you'll be following. The route has been recently waymarked (2023) with posts carrying white bands. Beyond the sign the track arcs hard to the left. On reaching a junction by a pylon, keep right and uphill, following white-banded marker posts. There are numerous side paths here, many created by mountain bikers, so it is best to simply follow the posted trail as it climbs, steeply in places, sometimes along a fire break with a line of pylons.

The path leads you through a wooden-posted stile then continues on a boardwalk through a thick stand of coastal shrub. Passing a second wooden-posted stile, you emerge from the thick undergrowth and once again enter the fire break where angling hard left for 50m, you reach a junction where a finger-post sign directs walkers to the left and horse riders to the right. Ignore the sign and go right along the horse route. Continue to follow white-banded marker posts across a more open section of ground, where you cross a (usually dry) stream via stepping stones.

After the stepping stones you reach a broad track. Continue straight over and up a concreted road with a 'No campervan' sign and another for El Tesorio. The track heads on up towards the jagged crest of the **Loma de San Bartolomé**. You pass an information board about the crest to your right. Bear left on the main track away from the crest, ignoring a track off to the right. On reaching a bank

Descent through pine forest on the approach to Playa de los Corrales

of green letterboxes for **Betijuelo**, turn right. The track now loops up through the trees, following white markers. At a three-way fork take the middle option, still following white markers.

Shortly you reach the broad ridge top where stone steps to the right lead up over the rock to a tubular trig point surrounded by a rectangular base, at 334m (**1hr 15min**). ◀

From this high **viewing point** you're treated to soaring views out west to the bay of Bolonia and east to the bay of Valdevaqueros. Descending the steps cut right towards the sea past a marker post, down a narrow path. Running down the left side of a fence, the path becomes more overgrown. At a point where the fence angles left, pass through a wire gate (always open), just right of a wooden-posted stile.

The path becomes sandier as it continues its descent through thick stands of broom: on a clear day the Moroccan coast and Jebel Musa are visible directly ahead. After crossing a dry stream, you pass through another stile beyond which you should angle right. Sticking close to the fence, the path cuts right, then once

The trig point is a geodetic vertex. These are used in conjunction with other vertices to form exact geographical positions of land masses mainly in regard to continental shift. This one is part of a system used to measure the ever changing distance (by millimetres) over time to Africa.

The walk along Punta Macotilla

Playa de los Corrales

more left, now running to the left of a wooden-posted railing, parallel to the (dry) bed of the **Arroyo de los Puercos**, still following white-marked posts.

Eventually the railing ends, at which point you reach the bed of the (dry) stream. Angling left then left again, the path angles slightly away from the stream before reaching a dirt track. Here cut left. Passing a number of houses and a parking area, the track runs up to the **A2325**. Here, passing a sign 'Fin de Sendero', angle right across the road and follow a stony track down towards the sea, signposted Playa 300m. The track narrows to become a sandy path that leads down to the beautiful beach of **Playa de Los Corrales** (**2hr 5min**).

Head down to the ocean's edge, where the firmer sand makes for easier walking. ▶ After passing beneath a pillbox you reach a rockier headland where, after clambering over rocks beneath a second pill box, you reach sand once more. Reaching a third pillbox angle away from the sea and cut through a small breach in the headland of **Punta Macotilla** at the western end of Valdevaqueros beach. Continue along the beach then angle left towards the first beach bar to return to the car park and your point of departure (**3hr**).

From here you might choose to walk barefoot back to Valdevaqueros beach.

73

WALK 7
Río de Guadalmesí circuit

Start/finish	The Área Recreativa El Bujeo next to the N-340 between Algeciras and Tarifa
Distance	6.5km
Ascent/descent	200m
Grade	Easy/Medium
Time	1hr 35min
Refreshments	None en route
Access	From Algeciras take the N-340 towards Tarifa. Pass Pelayo then, just beyond the pass of El Bujeo, at km95, turn right. Continue for 150m to an open area where there's parking and a signboard marking your route, Sendero Rio Guadalmesí SLA113. If approaching from the west, 1.5km after passing a petrol station turn left just before the pass of El Bujeo. The entrance to the *área recreativa* is very rough.

This easy, circular walk introduces you to the *canuto* ecosystem of the southern reaches of the Alcornocales Natural Park. The richly exuberant flora of the river and stream beds of the *canutos* is born of exceptionally warm and humid climatic conditions and is an ecosystem that is unique in southern Europe.

The walk begins close to the coastal road so expect to hear traffic for the first 20min or so. Once you cut inland things take on a much more peaceful, sylvan note as you follow a forestry track that loops lazily round the southern side of the Guadalmesí valley. Reaching the upper reaches of the river, you angle down into the river valley, where a beautiful path cuts through the lush *sotobosque* (the vegetation beneath the forest canopy, particularly lush in the southern valleys of the Alcornocales park), past huge sandstone borders, before angling back up to meet the track you followed earlier in the walk.

The walk begins at the Área Recreativo El Bujeo next to a signboard for Sendero Río Guadalmesí SLA113. Passing left of a huge eucalyptus, head away from the sign along a track that soon passes just right of Villa Pepe y Ana. After passing a number of houses the track angles further away

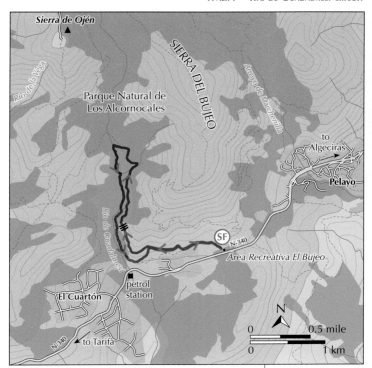

from the coastal road, climbing up through cork-oak forest as it skirts round the western flank of the **Sierra del Bujeo**. After passing a signboard about Torre Almenara Guadalmesí (which is visible to the south) the track arcs right, now running directly away from the sea, before crossing a **cattle grid**. The track continues steadily uphill.

At a point where the track begins to loop right, you reach a marker post with green and white bands on the left, along with a metal sign, El Cabrito-Puerto Bujeo and Rio Guadalmesi, on the right (40min). Here angle left, away from the track along a narrow path that crosses a more open swathe of land to reach a marker post. Here

Rocky descent next to Río Guadalmesí

angle hard left through the ferns and continue down a path close to the left bank of the **Río Guadalmesí**.

The **names of many Andalusian rivers** begin with 'Guad', like Guadalquivir, Guadalete, Guadiana and Guadalmesí. They are all of Moorish origin, being the Spanish pronunciation and spelling of the Arabic names that began with 'wadi' meaning 'river'.

The **Guadalmesí** is one of the shortest of the region's rivers, just 7km in length, and its prolific plant life is an excellent example of subtropical 'laurisilva' vegetation, which in mainland Spain is found only along the southern fringes of the Alcornocales park.

The path, marked with wooden posts with white arrows, angles away from the river then drops back down, closer to its course again. Leaving the river bed once more the path angles higher. ◄ Crossing a swathe of more open hillside, and climbing more steeply, you pass another signboard, 'Río Guadalmesí'. After running closer to the **N-340** and meeting with a wooden post-and-rail fence, the path cuts left and climbs steeply to reach the track you followed earlier, marked with white arrows. Here cut right and retrace your steps back to the start point (**1hr 35min**).

Views open out across the Strait to Morocco where, on clear days, Jebel Musa is clearly visible.

WALK 8

Pelayo circuit via the Torre de Guadalmesí

Start/finish	Parking area by the N-340, Pelayo, just next to a large sign made of white letters spelling out Algeciras
Distance	19km; 11km (shorter version)
Ascent/descent	600m
Grade	Medium/Difficult (complete walk); Medium (shorter version)
Time	5hr; 3hr (shorter version)
Refreshments	None en route
Access	From Algeciras take the N-340 in the direction of Cádiz. After approximately 5km you reach the hamlet of Pelayo. Here pull off the road at the signs for Complejo Rural Huerta Grande. Park by the large 'Bienvenido a Algeciras' sign. There are Sendero signs for the Colada de la Costa-Huerta Grande and the Cerro del Tambor. You will walk some of both of these routes.

This long, circular walk begins just outside the village of Pelayo. Early in the walk you follow a recently re-opened drovers' path that leads down to the Strait and the last reaches of the Mediterranean Sea. From here you follow a beautiful path along the ocean's edge to Guadalmesí, whose ancient watchtower once protected the Andalusian coastline from raids by North African corsairs. Parts of the path to the sea are overgrown. You might wish to pack some long trousers.

From here a broad dirt track angles steeply back inland to a line of wind turbines, from where a narrow track leads out to the abandoned military outpost of Cerro del Tambor. The views from this high promontory – across the Strait to Morocco and east and west along the Spanish coast – are a highlight of the walk. The hike can be shortened, and a long section of track avoided, by cutting inland at Cala Parra.

With your back to the large 'Bienvenido a Algeciras' sign, walk down the narrow tarmac lane signed Alojamiento Rural and Reception (for the Huerta Grande), shortly passing a 10kmh speed restriction sign. The lane jinks left at a gate then immediately back right. Just after the

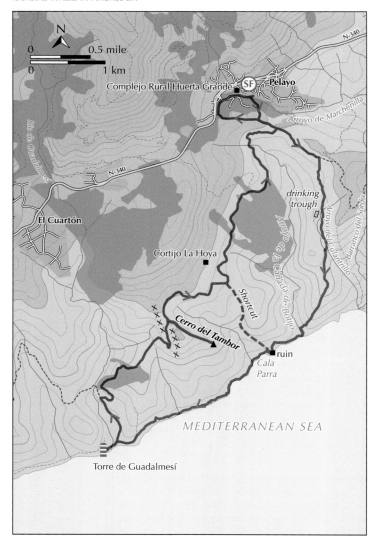

right jink look for a small wooden gate on your left. Go through this gate. If you arrive at the reception of Huerta Grande then you've overshot.

Descend along a narrow vegetated path to cross the stream, the **Arroyo de Marchenilla**, angling right, still on the narrow path, as it follows the stream bank. There are occasional wooden handrails. Shortly, look for a path off to your right that recrosses the stream. It's easy to miss; if you reach the village you've gone too far. After crossing the stream the path ascends past fences and private hunting signs. Shortly, you reach a metal stile, which you climb through somewhat awkwardly. After the stile you pass around to the left of a large, white agricultural building and reach a broad track. Here turn left.

Descend gently to a fork with a large pylon at its apex and a lone palm tree off to the left. Take the left fork but almost immediately bear right down a less distinct track for about 50m before it meets a much more defined track. Bear left onto this track. The track climbs gently then arcs left before running up to a marker post and a sign 'Recuperación de Vía Pecuaria La Marchenilla'. Here cut right along a less distinct track, heading directly towards the sea. You are now following part of the GR92, a new long-distance route, the Sendero Europeo Arco Mediterráneo, with red and white banded marker posts. The track descends and crosses a dry stream. Running gently uphill, the track reaches a long **drinking trough**. Here angle 45 degrees left and continue over a low rise. This path is very easy to miss and is somewhat overgrown.

The track narrows to become a footpath which shortly leads through a wire-and-post gate. Cutting right the path crosses a (dry) stream then arcs left once more and resumes its former course. As you climb, the path passes through two stiles as it runs on along the top of a ridge towards the sea then descends towards the Med'. Reaching the bed of the **Cañada de Botijo stream**, with its thick bower of vegetation, cut hard left still following the GR92. Do not be drawn ahead into the dense undergrowth around the stream. Many have and there are lots

Rocky strata seen from the path near Cala Parra

of false paths as a result. Once you have cut hard left, the path ascends briefly and veers away from the stream bed before backing to the right and descending to the beach (**1hr 10min**).

Turn right along the beach for 40m then angle right again up a path which climbs up between the low-growing coastal scrub then passes through a metal gate. The path runs above a pebbled beach then passes behind a **ruin**, beyond which there are twin benches. Here the path angles hard right and after 50m reaches a fork.

Shortcut
If you wish to shorten the walk you can cut right, following a sign for Huerta Grande. A narrow path cuts through the coastal scrub, heading directly away from the sea. After 375m the path widens to become a track as you pass to the right of a house. Continue up the track then, reaching a junction with a broader track, turn right and continue to **Cortijo La Hoya**.

Cutting left at a sign for Tarifa, the path angles down to the beach of Cala Parra. After 75m the path angles up to the right and resumes its course parallel to the sea. After cutting back down to the beach again the path again cuts inland. Passing to the left of a military stone hut, the path, occasionally braiding, passes through a metal gate. Some 30m beyond the gate you pass a ruined hut then descend to a stretch of pebbly beach. Continue along the beach for 50m then cut inland once more.

The path passes above a steep, eroded section of cliff where parallel strata of rock run out to the sea. Soon the Torre de Guadalmesí comes into sight. After crossing a (dry) stream bed the path leads through a green metal gate then angles left and returns to the water's edge. After 75m angle right up a run of sandy steps then head on through a ramshackle gate made of an old bed base.

After crossing more open ground you reach a fence where, passing through a stile and cutting left, the path widens then descends to a junction just inland from the bay of Guadalmesí (**2hr 20min**). Here cut left to reach the sea then follow a track which crosses the beach, fords the Guadalmesí, then loops steeply up to **Torre de Guadalmesí**.

After visiting the tower – it's a great spot to break for a picnic and, unusually for Andalucía, it has a picnic table – retrace your steps back to the junction you passed at 2hr

The beach and the tower at Torre de Guadalmesí

20min. Here turn left along a track which runs between the houses of Guadalmesí. After passing a cattle shed you reach a junction. Here cut right past a low building and get ready for a section of steep climbing. After passing through a glade of eucalyptus the track climbs up to a line of **wind turbines** where, just beyond a white hut where the specs of the turbines are detailed, you reach a junction. Cutting right, then after a few metres left, follow a narrow track southeast for 600m to reach the former gun emplacement at **Cerro del Tambor (3hr 55min)**.

Cádiz has more **wind turbines** than any other province in Spain, harnessing the winds that blow from both the Atlantic and the Mediterranean. Wind turbines supply 20% of Spain's electricity, compared with nuclear energy, which supplies 22%. The wind energy debate remains highly charged: many migrating birds are killed by the rotating blades as are large numbers of sedentary vultures. Some turbines are equipped with radar that detects the approach of birds then emits a warning sound, triggering a change in flight direction.

Retrace your steps back to the junction by the electricity hut then angle right and continue along the track, heading back towards Pelayo. It is now a track all the way to the finish. Passing farm gates where two china Dalmatians stand vigil, continue up the track. The track levels then loops further inland past the track cutting left to Cortijo La Hoya. ◀

The shortcut rejoins here.

After climbing gently in a more northerly direction the track eventually loops right and runs up to the junction with the track you followed earlier in the walk. Turn left, uphill, and follow the track up past the big, white agricultural building on your right that you will recall from earlier in the day. Here you could turn right and retrace your steps along the stream route back to the start. The broad track continues more or less straight uphill for some distance before angling right and then descending to your start point (**5hr**).

WALK 9
Río de la Miel circuit

Start/finish	To the west of the Barriada de El Cobre, at the locked gate to the track that leads to the Río de la Miel
Distance	11km
Ascent/descent	475m
Grade	Medium/Difficult
Time	3hr 20min
Refreshments	None en route
Access	From the A7 motorway take exit 105 for Algeciras Oeste/ Avda Agua Marina. Turn right at the first roundabout towards Barriada de El Cobre. After 200m bear left past Bar El Estribo, cross a railway line, then follow a winding road to a roundabout surrounded by palm trees. Exit along Calle Escritora Mariana Carvajal. The road bears right, running parallel to an aqueduct. Turn right at a sign 'Sendero Río de la Miel', passing beneath the aqueduct along Calle Maestra Luisa. After 350m turn left at a second sign 'Sendero Río de la Miel'. Park on the left after 50m.

Offering a superb introduction to the varied topography of the Alcornocales park, this circuit close to Algeciras numbers among the more challenging circuits in this guide. After heading inland by way of a broad forestry track the adventure begins as you follow a steep footpath up to a high ridge. Sticking close to the crest of the ridge you merge with La Ruta de las Prisioneros.

A narrow path then leads through dense oak forest to a ruined farm from where you drop steeply down to the Río de la Miel. Here you clamber across boulders to reach its northern bank from where you follow a narrow path down the course of the river, past a series of idyllic rock pools, to reach the Molino del Águila. Sections of the path are quite overgrown so it's worth packing long trousers or gaiters.

The walk begins at a signboard for Sendero Río de la Miel in front of a metal gate. From here head west along a broad track. Passing a set of metal gates to your right, you reach a

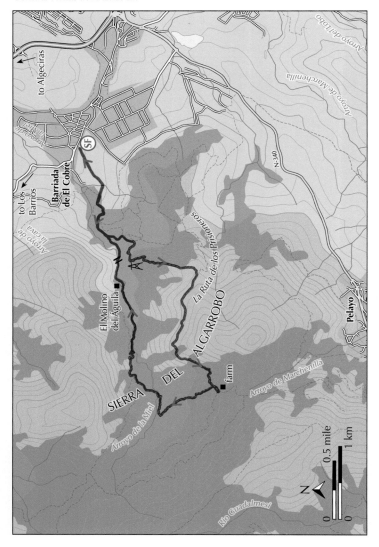

fork and a sign 'Parque Natural'. Here bear left and climb past another farm. The track winds on, levels, then climbs to a fork with an oak in its middle. Here turn left, ignoring white lettering on the tree pointing right for Río de la Miel.

After angling left then right the track passes a high **pylon**. Continue along the track for 125m then angle right along a narrow path which winds steeply up to the top of a ridge where it leads through a wire-and-post gate. Beyond the gate cut left and continue along the ridge top, parallel to the fence. Eventually, the path angles right and merges with a broad track, **La Ruta de los Prisioneros**.

> **La Ruta de los Prisioneros** was built by Republican prisoners during the 1940s at a time when Franco and the Nationalists feared that exiled Republicans might mount an attack from North Africa. The recent resurfacing of the track, with the subsequent burial of most of its cobbled surface, has been seen by many Spaniards as disrespectful to the 14,000 POWs who created this high mountain track through the Sierra del Algarrobo with their forced labour.

Angling right, you pass a ramshackle byre. The track climbs gently across an open swathe of land, passing a signboard for El Monte Comares then another one for Valle del Arroyo de la Miel. 150m beyond the second sign you pass just to the left of a bridge then reach a sign for Fin de Sendero.

Some 50m beyond the bridge cut right along a narrow, sandy path that laces its way between the trees, gradually bearing left. After a downhill section across an area that has seen a fire in the not-so-distant past the path enters a dense swathe of oak forest as it crosses over two (dry) stream beds then passes a round concrete pipe. Here the path angles right and climbs more steeply then levels as you reach a **ruined farm** festooned in greenery, just to the left of two huge eucalyptus trees. It makes a natural resting point (**1hr 40min**).

From here retrace your steps for 125m to a large cairn. Here cut left along a narrow path marked by cairns, which leads you all the way down to the Río de la Miel. The lower section of the path is less distinct as it angles right as it threads its way through thick beds of ferns. After zigzagging more steeply down you reach the river bed. Here, cutting across to its northern bank, you pick up another narrow path which soon angles away from the river.

Crossing two dry stream beds, the path reaches more open ground where it winds left towards a pylon, then once more right where it cuts through thicker vegetation. The path passes to the left of a small pylon then, crossing another (dry) stream, begins to descend.

Sections of metal pipe, which are partly buried beneath the path, can now be spotted.

The path is now cobbled in sections, running high above the Río de la Miel whose waters you'll hear down to your right. ◀ After cutting steeply down a more eroded section the path angles left before it passes just left of another pylon.

Waterfall and rock pool, Río de la Miel

Care is now required. Some 125m past the pylon (and about 10m before the path crosses a boulder-strewn stream bed where, to the left, there's a small, metal-spouted spring. If you see the metal-spouted spring you've come a few metres too far) you reach a solitary oak, clad in ferns at the top of its trunk. Here cut right past a table-shaped rock down an indistinct, overgrown path which after 20m cuts right then left once more before dropping down to the **Arroyo de la Miel**.

Reaching the river clamber across the rocks to its far bank (2hr 35min). Here you pick up a narrow path which descends parallel to the river, as you pass above a series of idyllic rock pools. Heading on down the river's right bank, the path follows the course of a metal water pipe which cuts down – you do the same – to cross the river at a point where, to your left, there's another beautiful rock pool.

Head on down the river's left bank, still following the metal water pipe. Reaching another rock pool, pass along its left edge then climb over a low wall that blocks the path. The path shortly passes a wooden barrier and a sign 'Fin de Sendero Río de la Miel'. Heading on past the ruined mill of **El Molino del Águila**, you pass a spring before crossing an arched **footbridge**. Bearing left past a white building, the path merges with a track that you should follow back to the junction with an oak at its midst. From here retrace your steps back to the walk's start point (**3hr 20min**).

WALK 10

Gibraltar circuit via Mediterranean Steps

Start/finish	Casemates Gate, Gibraltar
Distance	9.5km
Ascent/descent	500m
Grade	Medium
Time	2hr 50min
Refreshments	At the cable-car restaurant
Access	From the border cross the runway, following signs for City Centre. The walk begins in front of Casemates Gate and the tunnels leading to Casemates Square. A number 5 bus from the border will set you down directly in front of the gate.

It may come as a surprise to discover this mesmerising trail on Gibraltar, which numbers among the most spectacular on the Mediterranean Coast. The highlight of the walk – so long as you have a head for heights – is the extraordinary footpath that leads up the sheer, southern face of the Rock, known as Mediterranean Steps. This giddy path has recently been restored and you can't help but marvel at the derring-do of those who built it. And there are many more treats in store.

After negotiating the Steps, Douglas Path leads you along the top of Gibraltar's rugged spine, where huge views open out to the east and west. The next challenge comes in the form of Charles V Wall, which you descend via a series of steep flights of steps. A good head for heights is useful here as the steps are narrow and look straight down onto the town. Adding to the experience, there are often lazy Barbary macaques on the steps that are reluctant to make way.

There is a significant fee these days for entry to the area of the Rock and all of its attractions – £19 in 2024. It is probably best to plan for a long day looking at many of its other attractions to make the price worthwhile. Sadly, it's not possible to access the Mediterranean steps without paying. On the plus side, this is a spectacular and memorable walk. The Rock cable car, while not part of the walk, is another separate charge.

The walk begins in front of Casemates Gate. From here cut through two tunnels to reach Casemates Square.

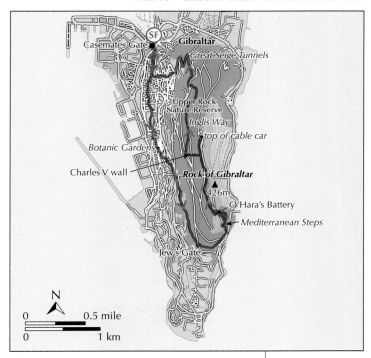

Angle right across the square then head along to the far end of Main Street. Passing John Macintosh Square then The Convent, pass beneath the arch of Southport Gates. Beyond the gate cut right across a pedestrian crossing, then bear left and traverse a second crossing. Angling left you reach the main entrance of the Queen's Hotel. Here cross the road, pass to the right of a restaurant to the lower station of the cable car then angle left across a car park to the gateway to the Gibraltar **Botanic Gardens** (**20min**).

Beyond the gate climb two flights of steps, pass a statue of Elliott, commander of the Rock during the Great Siege, then after 15m bear left up a narrow path.

> The **Great Siege of Gibraltar** (1779–1783) was an unsuccessful third attempt by the Spanish, aided by the French, to recapture the Rock. Lasting three years and seven months, it was the longest siege ever endured by British forces.

Climb another flight of steps then continue up Olive Tree Climb. This merges with a broader path that leads up to a red phone box. Here cut left at a sign 'Exit Upper Rock' and climb past the Rock Hotel's swimming pool. Passing through the gate to the gardens, continue parallel to Europa Road. Here cross the road and head up Engineer Road. The road climbs steeply to the gates of the Upper Rock Nature Reserve.

Continuing to climb, the road leads to another set of gates and a ticket box (**40min**) at the point known as **Jew's Gate** (where you pay 50 pence, or €1, to visit the Upper Rock area). Just beyond the ticket box is one of the hypothetical sites of the Pillars of Hercules, Mons Carpe. Angling left beyond the ticket box to a barrier, you reach the beginning of **Mediterranean Steps**.

> **Mediterranean Steps** were created by the Gibraltar garrison to link two of the Rock's most strategic points of defence: the gun emplacement next to Jew's Gate (180m) and O'Hara's Battery (426m). Other gun emplacements and military buildings dating back to World War II lie to either side of the path.

Passing a metal gate, you follow the steps along the near sheer face of Gibraltar's southern flank. Passing a signboard detailing the fauna of the Upper Rock, the path cuts left and climbs steeply: ropes help your upwardly mobile course. On reaching a bricked-up building (**1hr**) angle right through a tunnel beyond which you pass two bunkers: the views from the platform just beyond the second one are breathtaking.

After passing a group of antennae, you reach the highest point of the walk as vistas open out to the west. Along the ridge are various Rock attractions, which you could take extra time to visit, especially as you've paid for them.

Angling left, the path zigzags up to a signboard describing the Rock's unique flora. ◀ Angling left and descending, you reach the entrance gate to **O'Hara's**

Battery. Here cut right down a narrow road for 400m to a junction and sign '1789–1897' (**1hr 25min**). Here cut right past a barrier: you're now on Douglas Path, which angles up to the ridge top through thick Mediterranean scrub and reaches another gun battery.

Continue along the spine of the Rock, now descending, to St Michael's Road. Angling right here you pass a signboard telling of a Spanish attack on the Rock in 1704. Continue along the road then pass beneath an arch where Gibraltar's resident apes gather to look at tourists.

Looking north along the Rock from the Mediterranean Steps

> The colony of **rock apes** or Barbary macaques (*Macacus sylvanus*) is the only wild monkey population in Europe. There are some 300 macaques in all, living in five different troops. The macaques were present on the Rock at the time it was ceded to Britain and it's generally accepted that the original apes came with the Moors from North Africa. Legend holds that Gibraltar will remain under British dominion until macaques disappear from the Rock.

Beyond the arch you reach the top of **Charles V Wall**. Continue up St Michael's Road, angle right at the first fork then climb to the **top station of the cable car** where there's a café and a viewing platform up to the right: close encounters of the ape kind are guaranteed, as well as mesmerising views of Africa and the western end of the Costa del Sol (**1hr 40min**).

Retrace your steps to the top of Charles V Wall then cut right and make your way down the first section of wall. Cutting right then left, drop down its second section. Cut right at a brick building then left through a gate and continue down the third section of wall to a picnic area. Exit onto Queen's Road where, just opposite, you'll see a sign **Inglis Way**. Follow the path up then over a flight of wooden steps past a barrel-roofed brick hut.

Some 15m before reaching a tarmac road the path cuts left and threads its way through thick Mediterranean scrub. Passing above two abandoned buildings, you reach a wooden platform in front of a fence. Here angle right. The path climbs then arcs left, parallel to a low wall. Angling left and descending across two metal pipes, you come to a road (**2hr 15min**).

Cut left for 50m then angle right along Queen's Road. On reaching a 'Give way' sign continue straight on towards the entrance to the **Great Siege Tunnels**, angle left down Willis's Road for 200m then loop hard right. After 150m, angling once more left, you pass the Moorish castle. Reaching twin Give Way signs head straight on for 50m to a bus stop then cut right and down Castle Steps.

At the next junction head straight on, still descending the steps, following signs for City Centre. At the bottom of the steps continue down Bell Lane to reach Main Street once again. From here retrace your steps to the start point of the walk (**2hr 50min**).

Residents of the Rock, (Barbary Apes)

2 COSTA DEL SOL

The eastern face of La Crestellina near Casares (Walk 12)

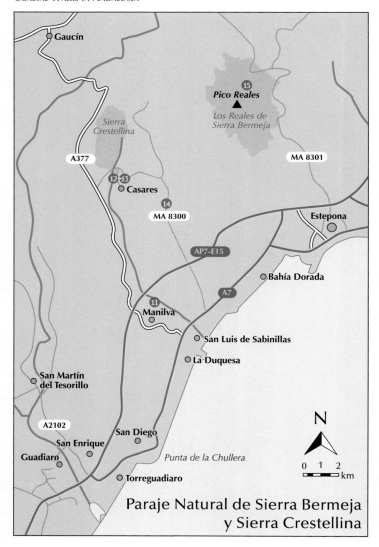

Gaucín

Sierra
Crestellina

A377

12-13
Casares

14
MA 8300

Pico Reales
Los Reales de
Sierra Bermeja
15

MA 8301

Estepona

AP7-E15

A7

Bahía Dorada

11
Manilva

San Luis de Sabinillas

La Duquesa

San Martín
del Tesorillo

A2102

San Diego

San Enrique

Guadiaro

Punta de la Chullera

Torreguadiaro

N

0 1 2
km

Paraje Natural de Sierra Bermeja
y Sierra Crestellina

PARAJE NATURAL DE SIERRA BERMEJA Y SIERRA CRESTELLINA

Grazing sheep in the Sierra Bermeja (Walk 15)

The deep-red mountainside of Sierra Bermeja – it means 'vermilion massif' – is as unmistakable a landmark of the western Costa del Sol as the shell-like form of La Concha is further to the east. The high magnesium and iron content of its peridotite rocks accounts for its colour and strangely lunaresque aspect: seen at dawn or dusk the mountain seems to glow like a red lantern above the sea. Over the millennia what once were volcanic cones and craters have been gradually rounded off to give the mountains their present aspect, even though the peak of Los Reales, a mere 7.5km back from the sea, still towers up to almost 1500m.

The region's unusual geology, coupled with it being subject to weather systems coming from both the Atlantic and Mediterranean, have given rise to a diverse plants and wildlife, with a number of endemic species. The botanical jewel of the sierra is its stand of pinsapos, an arboreal relic from the Ice Age, which was first documented by the Swiss botanist Boissier, from whom its full Latin name, *Abies pinsapo boiss*, derives. The Pico Reales circuit (Walk 15) leads you through the dramatic forest of pinsapos, which is recovering incredibly well after a huge fire in August 2021, before it passes to the southern sea-facing flank of the mountain.

The wildlife of Sierra Bermeja is similarly rich in species and this is among the best spots in southern Spain for the observation of raptors. The jagged ridge of the Sierra Crestellina, just west of Los Reales, is home to a large colony of griffon vultures. Since the birds became a protected species a number of feeding sites have been established, and the Casares circuit (Walk 14) takes you past one of these avian fast-food outlets.

Bonelli's, golden and booted eagles are all present in the area, along with eagle owls, Egyptian vultures, peregrine falcons and kestrels. The sierra is also home to a large number of Egyptian mongoose – it was here that they were first recorded outside Africa – as well as the rare corzo morisco (*Capreolus capreolus*), a sub-species of roe deer that has adapted to the warmer conditions of this southernmost part of Europe and whose coat is quite different to that of its Spanish cousins.

At the edge of this huge swathe of volcanic magma the extraordinary rock formations of the Sierra de Utrera are very different. The deeply weathered fissures and fantastic forms of its karst limestone are a match for those of the better-known Torcal de Antequera, and the path that cuts through the Canuto de la Utrera gorge is among the most spectacular geological excursions in southern Spain. Towards the end of this circuit (Walk 11) you pass Los Baños de Hedionda, where you can still take a dip in the hot sulphurous baths that have been known since Roman times for their curative properties.

On all walks described in this section you can expect big ocean views across the Bay of Algeciras to Gibraltar, and on clear days across the Strait to the mountains and villages of the northernmost swathe of Morocco.

A large swathe of the park to the east and northeast of Picos Reales was affected by the devastating forest fire of September 2021, including the first few hundred metres of Walk 15 between the signboard at the walk's start point and the ceramic sign about the poet Lorca.

WHERE TO STAY

Casares should be your first choice if you're overnighting in the area, a quintessentially Andaluz village wrapped round a jagged peak, complete with a Moorish castle and an organic cluster of white houses. Manilva is pretty untainted by tourism but its one hostel might be a touch basic for some tastes. But there's a reliable Costa alternative in nearby Sabanillas. For hotel listings see Appendix B.

MAPS

All five walks in the area are covered by IGN 1:50,000 Jimena de la Frontera 1071 (14–46) . For Walk 15 the extra detail of the 1:25000 1071–II is useful.

TAXIS

Manilva tel 952 80 29 00
Casares tel 670 88 43 94
Estepona tel 952 80 29 00
Sabanillas tel 952 802 900

WALK 11
Manilva circuit via the Utrera Gorge

Start/finish	Villa Los Álamos, near Manilva
Distance	10km
Ascent/descent	445m
Grade	Medium
Time	3hr 5min
Refreshments	None en route
Access	From Sabanillas follow the A377 to Manilva. Here follow signs for Centro Urbano then turn right at a sign for the AP7 Málaga/Algeciras/Cádiz. Head round the east side of the village to a point where the road doglegs left then right. Here cut right down Calle Padre Mariano. Follow this road to the bottom of the hill then turn left. Pass the Roman Oasis restaurant then just before the towering motorway bridge cut right on a track. Continue for 150m until you see a small house, Villa Los Álamos (formerly a restaurant), tucked away on the right on the other side of the stream. There is lots of space to park along the left side of the track.

The deeply weathered karst formations of the Utrera Gorge, the southernmost of their kind in Europe, number among western Málaga's most remarkable natural features. Home to Bonelli's eagles, as well as Egyptian vultures, the gorge is a fine example of the *canuto* (or gorge) ecosystem that is unique to this part of Andalucía.

There are more treats in store: a beautiful path leading down the Río Manilva past a series of ancient mill houses, soaring views out to Casares and down to the Mediterranean, as well as the fascinating Hedionda baths, which since Roman times have attracted visitors to their hot, sulphurous waters. These all amply compensate for the stretch of road walking at the western end of the gorge. Parts of the path along the Río Manilva are quite overgrown so pack long trousers or gaiters, and remember to take a bathing costume if you wish to immerse yourself in the Hedionda baths.

From Villa Los Álamos head north along a broad track for 300m to a signboard on the left 'Sendero local Canuto

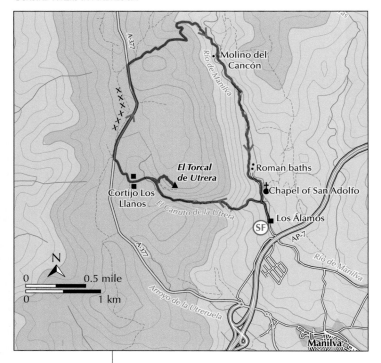

de la Utrera' marking **El Canuto de la Utrera**. Here cut left on a narrow footpath that leads into the mouth of the Utrera gorge through thick stands of oleander, at first following the left-hand bank of the *canuto*. Crossing to the northern bank the path leads you to the area known as **El Torcal de Utrera**, a remarkable swathe of karst limestone that rises to both sides of the stream. In parts the path is made up of huge slabs of limestone. Green and white waymarking leads you through the gorge past stands of oleander, wild olive, carob, lentiscus and fan palm. ◄ The gorge widens as it reaches twin concrete water deposits (**25min**).

You occasionally need to use hands as well as feet as you clamber between the rocks.

Karst topography is the result of the action of acid, created by the interaction of rainfall and CO_2, on a bedrock of limestone, dolomite or gypsum. Over time fissures gradually open in the rock, while many of the surface features of karst scenery, like sink holes and ravines, are caused by the collapse of similarly weathered, subterranean rocks.

There are fine views back along the gorge to the Med'. The floor of the gorge becomes broader and flatter as the path climbs before widening to become a track where you reach an information board about La Sierra de la Utrera. The track runs gently uphill towards a line of wind turbines and a tall red and white radio antenna. Reaching the top of the rise (**1hr 15min**), just as a farm comes into sight up ahead of you, cut right up a narrow path that immediately angles hard round to the right, marked with green paint splashes.

Some 15m after passing a stone bench angle left and continue climbing up through the rocks looking for the clearest path and blue paint splashes. ▶ After taking in the views retrace your steps back to the junction where you left the track (**1hr 45min**).

Reaching the top of the Torcal de Utrera there are no paths as such, but it's easy to clamber over the flat-topped rocks to find a good vantage point and a rest stop.

Karst formation in the Utrera Gorge

Turning right along the track, you shortly pass between two white buildings of **Cortijo Los Llanos**. Bearing sharply right, then left once more, the track crosses a cattle grid before running up to meet the **A377**. Here turn right and prepare yourself for a 1.3km stretch of road walking, parallel to the line of **windmills** to your left. Some 50m past the km9 post turn right along a broad dirt track. Passing a sign for Club Ecuestre Espiritú del Viento, after 125m you reach a fork. Take the right option. Passing an area of quarried sandstone Casares comes into view and, to the northwest, the Sierra Bermeja. The track begins to loop downwards as the Med' again comes into view.

On reaching a junction, ignore a track which angles hard left: stick to your course and follow a line of telegraph poles down towards the valley floor. Passing between two white gate pillars the track runs towards a concrete ford across **Río de Manilva**. 30m before the ford cut right along a less distinct track then after 50m cross the river via a footbridge. Beyond the bridge the path angles right, passes the ruined mill house of **Molino del Cancón**, then climbs and cuts through a gate (**2hr 15min**).

The path, overgrown on this section, runs on parallel to the river's left bank: look for PR waymarking. To

The oleander-lined bed of the Río Manilva

your right, more spectacular karst formations are visible as Manilva comes into view to the south. Looping round a landslide, the path drops down to the river, which you cross via stepping stones. Beyond the river, angling right, the path passes just right of a huge fig tree then arcs left and resumes its course parallel to the river's right bank. Passing a stand of eucalyptus it crosses the river again before looping back to the right bank.

On reaching a fence around a mill and a sign 'Prohibido el Paso' the path cuts once again to the left bank then, passing beneath a rocky overhang where an enormous boulder spans the river bed, cuts back to the opposite bank. Here it angles up to merge with a broader path which, after 50m, cuts right through the undergrowth to reach a wide track (**2hr 35min**). ▸

Be aware that there's also a waymarked path closer to the river but this leads across private land.

Bearing left along the track, Manilva comes into view as you pass above a ruined mill house then a recreational area with a swimming pool. Descending through a set of metal gates, you reach a broader track. Bearing right, you'll soon spot a number of steep paths cutting down to the left, which lead down to the **Roman baths** of La Hedionda. You may, or may not, be tempted to take a dip in their hot, sulphurous waters, which smell of rotten eggs, but curiously less so once you are in the water.

> The **Hedionda baths** date from the 1st century BC. Legend has it that Caesar, when governor of Spain, took the waters here. The waters have a high sulphur content and are said to be efficacious in the treatment of skin complaints. There are a number of clear pools ideal for paddling or dipping, plus a covered bath where you stoop through a rocky arch to enter a small roofed bathing chamber.

Passing a line of bins, continue down the valley on a path which runs parallel to the river's right bank then angle back up to the track you left earlier. Here you pass the buildings of the old spa then the **Chapel of San Adolfo**. Crossing the bed of the Canuto de Utrera, the track leads back to your point of departure (**3hr 5min**).

WALK 12
Casares circuit via La Crestellina

Start/finish	The main square in Casares, La Plaza de España
Distance	10km; 12km if climbing Cerro de las Chapas
Ascent/descent	550m; or 720m if climbing Cerro de las Chapas
Grade	Medium; Medium/Difficult if climbing Cerro de las Chapas
Time	3hr 15min; 4hr 30min if climbing Cerro de las Chapas
Refreshments	None
Access	Casares is easily found, situated 1km off the main A377 road that runs north from the coast at Manilva to Gaucin. Park at the main town multi-storey car park and follow the signs take take you in a loop above the town. The pedestrian exit is on the top level of the car park..

The hilltop village of Casares, just a few kilometres inland from the Mediterranean, numbers among the most dramatically situated villages in Andalucía and is worth an excursion in its own right. To the south of the village there are vast views out towards Gibraltar and Morocco, while to the north the jagged spine of the Sierra Crestellina, which has Paraje Natural status, provides a stunning backdrop to Casares' organic cluster of whitewashed buildings.

If you want a more challenging walk, don't miss the optional extension which leads up to the summit of Cerro de las Chapas. You may well spot ibex as you cut round the eastern flank of the Crestellina and will certainly see vultures riding the thermals as you approach the southern end of the ridge.

The walk begins in the Plaza de España, the main square of Casares, next to a line of benches. With your back to the benches bear left across the square then, passing right of bar La Bodeguilla de Enmedio, head up Calle Monde past a 'No entry' sign to the road, which runs round the top of the village. Bearing left after 50m, you reach information boards for Sendero local SL1 Sierra Crestellina and Stage 29 of the GR249. Here cut right up a steep concrete road whose surface soon changes to tarmac.

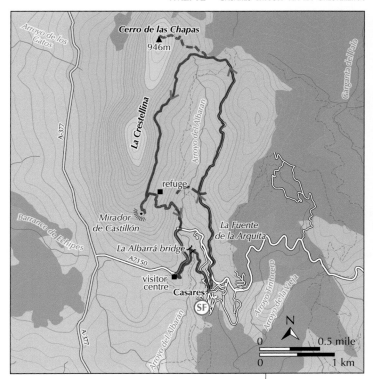

Soon you pass a spring (**La Fuente de la Arquita**) opposite a huge eucalyptus. ▸ Where the tarmac ends carry on along the main track, which cuts through thick stands of oak and pine forest with dense undergrowth, evidence of the high rainfall to which the area is subject. Soon you pass an area on the right where quarrying has taken place.

After passing Puerto de las Viñas, cork oaks begin to give way to pines. Some 200m past the farm, on reaching a fork, ignore a concreted track that cuts up to the right and stick to your same course and take the left fork. After

Soaring views open out to the west and to the eastern flank of the Crestellina as you climb on up past a number of houses and villas.

40m you reach another fork: here again take the left-hand option. After 200m you reach another fork and a second sign for Sendero Crestellina Natural. Here, bearing left, and deviating from the GR waymarking, you pass a green metal barrier.

The narrow forestry track climbs steeply as views open out to the east. To the left is a bench and a signboard on birds, where the views to the south are outstanding. Reaching the top of a rise and another marker post topped with a white arrow you come to another fork (**1hr 15min**). Here you have a choice.

To climb Cerro de las Chapas

If you wish to climb Cerro de las Chapas (it will take about an hour and a half to get up and down) cut right on a narrow track that winds through the pines to the base of the cliff. From here cut hard left on a steep, loose footpath marked with blue splashes of paint and the occasional cairn. The path weaves its way to the ridge top passing a small concrete hut, which was the base for an old transmitter mast. From here you'll need to take a few hand holds if you wish to climb to the highest point. Care should be taken when negotiating the sections of scree, especially on your descent.

From the ridge, follow the same path back to the junction.

If you prefer not to climb Cerro de las Chapas, keep left. The track gently descends as it loops round the bowl of the valley as views open out to the south: on clear days Gibraltar and North Africa are visible. The rocky crest of **La Crestellina** is now to your right. On reaching a point where the forestry track arcs hard left, look for a rocky path off to the right (**1hr 55min**). Cut right along the rocky path.

> Andalucía has several sedentary colonies of **griffon vultures** (*Gyps fulvus*). These enormous raptors, with a wingspan of over 2.5m, can weigh up to 10kg. It's estimated that there are some 3000 pairs in Andalucía. The vultures' favoured sites for colonisation are inaccessible, near-vertical cliff faces of 50m in height or more. Griffon vultures cover between 50 and 300km daily in their search for carrion.

Beyond an old sign the path angles left then climbs steeply to the end of a bluff and the **Mirador de Castillón**. ▶ Retrace your steps back to the point where you cut up to the *mirador*, turn right, and continue your descent. After approximately 200m you reach the back wall of a mountain **refuge**. Passing to the right of the refuge you'll spot a marker post that marks the continuation of the path, which loops steeply down to the valley floor. Take care: the path is loose in parts.

Reaching a fence, the path angles right before dropping down to a dirt track. Here go right. After 25m you reach a junction where, cutting right, you cross the concreted bed of Arroyo del Albarán, beyond which the track descends to meet the **A7150**. Cross the road and then turn right along a balustraded path lined with solar lamps. At a point where the road bears sharply right you

From here there are soaring views across the valley and, beyond, to the Sierra de Bermeja.

COASTAL WALKS IN ANDALUCÍA

reach the **Casares visitor centre**, El Centro de Visitantes (**3hr 5min**).

Cut left off the road then angle hard left along a concrete road, which passes just to the left of the visitor centre. The track drops steeply down to the valley floor, where it crosses the medieval **La Albarrá bridge**, then bears right and climbs to the first of the village houses, beyond which you pass a map of local footpaths. Heading straight along Calle Carrera you pass La Casa Natal de Blas Infante, which doubles as a tourist office.

> A free thinker and liberal of the 19th century, **Blas Infante** was born in Casares. He was a passionate defender of regional government and is known as 'El Padre de al Patria Andaluza' or 'The Father of Andalusian Nationalism'. Infante, along with other left-wing intellectuals, was executed by Franco's Nationalist insurgents when they took Sevilla in 1936.

Casares, seen from near the Mirador de Castillón

Reaching a square, open to its right side, head straight on to return to the main square of **Casares**, La Plaza de España (**3hr 15min**).

WALK 13

Casares eastern circuit

Start/finish	The main square of Casares, La Plaza de España
Distance	10.5km
Ascent/descent	530m
Grade	Medium
Time	3hr
Refreshments	None en route
Access	Casares is easily found, situated 1km off the main A377 road that runs north from the coast at Manilva to Gaucin. Park at the main town multi-storey car park and follow the signs take take you in a loop above the town. The pedestrian exit is on the top level of the car park.

This second Casares circuit combines two of the walking routes that have been marked out by the Casares town hall. They have been linked together to make a more interesting half-day excursion and to avoid their long sections of walking on tarmac. The route takes in the forested hillsides to the northeast of the village and the open farmland to its south, while for most of the walk you're treated to fine panoramic views of the Campo de Gibraltar, the Sierra Bermeja and, when the weather is clear, the mountains of the Moroccan Rif.

Be prepared for a steep final climb up to the village from the point where you cross the Tocón stream: its waters once powered the mill houses you pass as you head back towards the village.

The final stage of the walk leads you past Casares' unfinished cemetery which has lain abandoned for many years. It's a grim monument to the profligacy that has marked local municipal government in Andalucía during the past decades.

The walk begins in the Plaza de España, the main square of Casares, next to a line of benches. With your back to the benches angle left and pass just to the right of the steak restaurant, Bodeguilla de Enmedio. Take the first right along Calle Copera, which leads up past Hotel Rural de Casares. At the next fork keep left, climb a flight of steps then cut left up a narrow, paved, very steep street to meet the main road **MA8300**. Cutting right, past the Mi Cortijo restaurant, after 125m you reach a sign 'Ruta Circular La Manga/Celima/Arroyo Hondo'.

After 125m you reach a track off to the left, where there is an informative walk signboard, a finger post directional marker and a small concrete structure with a blue door. Take this track, which is quite new and leads initially past some ugly dog pounds and random sheds. At a point where the ugly track goes hard left uphill, carry straight on up a narrow path along the dry stream bed.

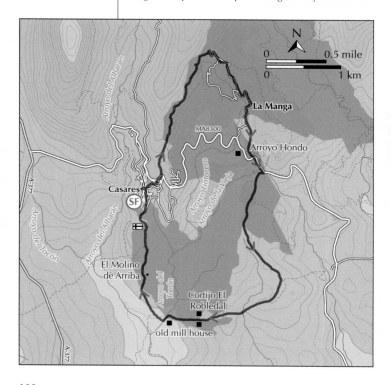

The path leading out from the village

Ignore a sign to the bird observatory. The path meets with a tarmac road and, angling left and climbing for 40m, you reach a fork.

Take the right fork and continue climbing along a broad track following a line of pylons. Ignore a track to the right signed Villa Camilla and keep left uphill. After passing above a number of houses the track narrows to become a path, which runs on through a stand of deciduous oaks. ▶ Reaching more open ground, the path shortly angles right then meets with a broad track (**40min**).

Bear right along the track, which shortly begins to descend through a swathe of cork oaks. After some 150m you reach a junction. Turn right, following a wooden finger sign 'SL-3 Celina'. The track, now concreted, loops past a water deposit. At the next junction you will see a sign to the left for Hotel Hermitage and Villa Essencia, along with a concrete hut with a metal door and a 'fire hydrant' sign. Here take the left option, maintaining your course straight on.

Views open out towards Estepona and the sea.

The track ascends gently, becoming prettier, through woodland with some large villas to your right. Now the track briefly becomes a narrow path as you pass close to a villa boundary wall then descend part of its concrete drive to join another track. Here bear right and continue, passing La Casa de Aguilla before reaching another track, where you keep right. Reaching the main road, **MA8300**, by a sign 'The Forge restaurant', turn left and walk 100m to a layby, with recycling bins, on the right. Go past the bins and cut up the ascending track with GR249 waymarking.

The **GR249** or '**Gran Senda de Málaga**' is a long-distance footpath that describes a 650km loop

The white-washed back streets of Casares

through Málaga province. At its eastern end it links in with the early stages of a variant of El Camino de Santiago, the 'mozarabic' route.

The concrete ends as the track runs on between cork oaks. On reaching a three-way junction, head straight on. After 325m you reach a fork. Again, branch left, following GR249 waymarking. The panorama is somewhat marred by pylons but shortly these cut away to the left and, following a high ridge towards the sea, the vistas improve as Gibraltar comes into view.

On reaching a fork (**2hr**), cut right, following a sign 'Casares 4km'. The track cuts across open fields, passes a group of farm buildings, then becomes rougher underfoot as it descends between hedgerows then crosses a (dry) stream bed. Passing a wooden-posted corral, the track once more descends as spectacular views open up towards Casares. The track passes between the twin gates of the **Cortijo El Robledal horse stud**.

The path, more overgrown, continues its descent, crosses a water channel then leads you through a green metal gate. Here the path angles left, past an **old mill house** then cuts right once more then crosses the stream bed of **Arroyo del Tocón** (**2hr 35min**). You may have to paddle at certain times of the year. Here bear right up a broad track, whose ancient cobbles are visible, towards Casares.

You reach another junction with a broader track. Here cut right, following a sign 'Casares 1.9km', and steel yourself for a hard climb. The track leads past an old mill, **El Molino de Arriba**, whose race is still visible at its right -hand side. The concreted track climbs steeply past the village's ghastly, unfinished **cemetery**. A steep final pull leads you past a signboard for El Camino de Jimena to a fork.

▶ Take the left fork and continue up into the village along Calle de Juan Cerón to return to the Plaza de España (**3hr**).

There are two via ferrata routes here high up into the cliffs on the left, and a very long, exhilarating zip wire ride high above your head, running from one side of the cliffs to the other.

WALK 14

Casares circuit via La Acedía

Start/finish	The walkers' signboard for La Acedía - Pasada del Pino, near Caseres
Distance	12km
Ascent/descent	500m
Grade	Medium
Time	3hr 15min
Refreshments	None en route
Access	From the coastal road take the MA8300 towards Casares. Some 50m past the km8 post look for a sign to the right for La Acedía and a signboard for Pasada del Pino/La Acedía. Turning right from the road, the track is plenty wide enough to leave your vehicle a few metres along on the right.

The Sierra Bermeja has a stark beauty all its own, and this longish walk leading to a beautiful rock pool in the upper reaches of the Garganta de las Acedias makes a great introduction to its lunaresque landscapes and the vermilion rock formations after which it is named.

The walk leads you past El Muladar de Casares, one of several sites in the southern sierras where carcasses are laid out for the resident colonies of griffon vultures. These enormous, carrion-eating birds are a protected species and numbers have increased massively since the sites were set up. If this sounds too macabre for your liking, by quickening your pace you can be past the site in seconds.

The early and later parts of the walk, which lead past a number of houses hidden away in leafy stands of oak, stand in marked contrast to the harsher landscapes of the middle section of the walk.

From the signboard for Pasada del Pino/La Acedía head away from the MA8300. After 30m concrete gives way to dirt track and you shortly pass a sign with a map of the route you'll follow.

Ignoring three tracks that cut off to the right (the second with a sign 'Tierra Buena'), follow the main track as it loops down through a swathe of cork oaks to a stand of eucalyptus trees, where it crosses a bridge over the (dry) stream bed of the **Garganta del Palo**. The track winds on past the entrance to Finca La Serena then crosses another (dry) watercourse. Bearing left, the track continues to ascend as it passes the oleander-lined boundary of **Casa Isabel** then reaches a triple fork (**35min**).

Here take the left option. The track arcs hard left before entering an area of sparser vegetation. The jagged ridge of La Crestellina comes into view to the northwest as the track leads you through a galvanised metal gate. After

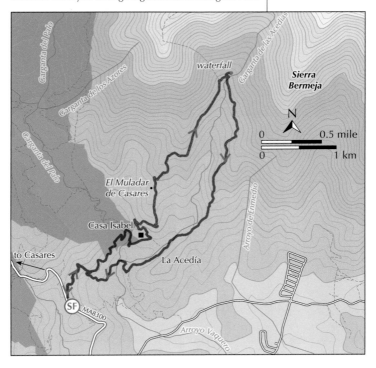

The pool in the Garganta de las Acedias

a few metres it arcs back right as views open out towards Estepona and the Med'. You pass a sign away to your left for Red Andaluza de Comederos de Aves Caroñeras and a fenced enclosure, **El Muladar de Casares**.

A **muladar** is a designated site where animal carcasses are laid out for birds of prey. This is part of an initiative to preserve existing vulture populations, which have seen a sharp decline in carrion due to the reduced numbers of flocks and the disappearance of beasts of burden from the sierras. Just 75 years ago many village homes would have had a donkey, horse or mule for working the land and transporting goods to local markets.

As you climb higher Gibraltar and, on clear days, Morocco come into sight.

◄ Bearing hard left, the track divides next to a concreted storm drain. Take the right fork, following green and white waymarking. The track runs northeast towards the head of the valley, high above the Garganta de las Acedias, whose waters you'll hear down beneath you. After passing just above a water trough the track angles right, crosses a (dry) watercourse then after 150m reaches the **Garganta de las Acedias** (**1hr 55min**).

> Some 15m before reaching the stream it's worth making a short diversion by taking the rough track which cuts off to the left. Following it for some 150m, as it arcs left then back right, you reach a **waterfall** and a rock pool reached by scrambling down the steep bank of the Acedias. When walked in 2024 extensive work was taking place on the stream crossing and surrounding tracks, making access to the pool difficult. Speaking with the Media Ambiente (park police), the intention is to restore the site after works are completed. A new pool has also been built just a few metres left of the crossing. It's a beautiful place

La Acedía and the western flank of the Sierra Bermeja

to break for a picnic and a dip in the stream. After visiting the rock pool retrace your steps to the point where you left the track.

At this stage, high above the track over to your right, the crumpled fuselage of a light aircraft is visible, which crashed on the mountainside in December 1998.

A few metres after crossing the stream you reach the highest point of the walk (approximately 550m) as the track arcs back towards the sea. ◄

The track continues onwards, veering gently right and on towards the sea, and begins to descend. As the track becomes less distinct look for a narrow path off to the right with green and white paint splashes. Take this path as it follows a spur ridge line before descending steeply. It's loose footing in parts.

The path descends to meet the track you left earlier. Go right and continue to descend through a swathe of pines, reaching a junction with a broad dirt track.

On the descent you will become increasingly aware of a massive rubbish recycling plant away down to your left. The huge diggers and tippers look tiny on the vast site. At the junction there is a signboard that gives details about the new plant – La Gestión de Residuos en la Costa del Sol Occidental. It takes in waste (mainly 'black bin' rubbish) from 11 municipalities. From the signboard go right and continue your descent.

Here, ignoring GR247 waymarking pointing left, bear right and continue your descent back towards the houses of **La Acedía**, shortly passing the entrance gates of Villa Bermeja. Continue down the main track, which is shaded in parts by ancient cork oaks. Passing a newly renovated house, you reach a junction. Here turn right. The track runs past more gated villas then arcs left past a paddock.

At the next junction cut right and cross the Acedias via a concrete bridge. After running on parallel to the river the track angles right, now climbing steeply, to eventually reach the track you followed earlier in the walk by the sign for Tierra Buena. Here cut left and retrace your steps back to the start point of the walk (**3hr 15min**).

WALK 15

Pico Reales circuit via El Pinsapar forest

Start/finish	The signboard for the Paseo de los Pinsapos, near Estepona
Distance	7km
Ascent/descent	350m
Grade	Easy/Medium
Time	2hr 30min
Refreshments	El Refugio, near the end of the walk
Access	From Estepona take the MA8301 towards Jubrique (it begins next to the Mercadona supermarket on the north side of the town) for 14.2km to the top of the pass, Puerto de Peñas Blancas. Here turn left past a sign for Los Reales, pass a green barrier then continue for 2.75km to a signboard to the right of the road, marking the beginning of the Pinsapo walk, Paseo de los Pinsapos.

This circular walk leads you to the highest point of the Sierra Bermeja Paraje Natural, the peak of Los Reales. Although just 8km inland from the Mediterranean, this mighty vermilion massif rises to 1452m and from its antennae-topped peak there's an extraordinary panoramic vista of a huge slice of Andalucía: north to the Genalguacíl valley and the Sierra de las Nieves, east to the Sierra de Ojén and La Concha, west to La Crestellina and the last reaches of the Alcornocales and south to Gibraltar, the Strait and Africa.

In 2021 a huge fire engulfed the Picos and surrounding municipalities. It was one of the largest blazes in living memory. Over 3000 homes were evacuated, while 4761 firefighters fought the fire along with fire planes and helicopters. Tragically, firefighter Carlos Martinez Haro lost his life. A moving memorial now stands in his honour towards the end of the walk.

While the fire caused enormous amounts of damage, the recovery in the flora along the route has been remarkable. In parts, the juxtaposition of the newer life against the older trees adds a unique beauty. Do not underestimate this walk for its relatively short distance and duration; it is remarkable. The road up to the start point is both jaw dropping and stunning.

From the signboard 'Paseo de los Pinsapos' head down a narrow, rocky path, which drops away from the road

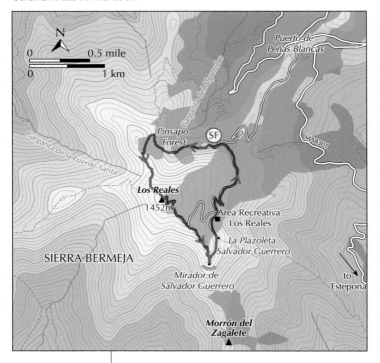

into the **Pinsapo Forest** then, levelling, passes a signboard about pinsapos. Some 50m after crossing a concrete bridge, look for a ceramic sign of a poem by Lorca inspired by the trees. Here cut left off the main path. The path climbs steeply through dense undergrowth: as you climb higher Mediterranean pines begin to take the place of the pinsapo pines.

The **pinsapo** (*Abies pinsapo*), often referred to as Spanish fir, is a rare species of tree that is found in only four mountainous areas of southern Spain and two in the north of Morocco. The trees favour north-facing slopes between 1100m and 1700m in height

The eastern flanks of Los Reales with fire-damaged trees

with mild yet wet climatic conditions. The trees were first catalogued by the Swiss botanist Pierre Edmond Boissier in 1838: you pass a plaque dedicated to him towards the end of the walk.

Some 30m after crossing a scree slope and boulder field cut sharp left and continue your ascent, zigzagging up through the pines and the reddish rocks. Marker posts lead up to a small breach in the rocks, beyond which you reach the top of the ridge, where views open out to the southwest and the Bay of Algeciras (**40min**).

Here the path bears left towards the antennae atop Los Reales peak before cutting back to the ridge's eastern side. Crossing the ridge once more, the path leads past a signboard about the mountain's peridotite rocks. Reaching a flatter area and bearing left it runs on up to the antennae. On reaching a white hut, cut right, pass a second hut, then follow a narrow path to the trig point marking the top of **Los Reales** (**1hr 5min**). ▶

This is a great spot to take a break and gulp in the incredible panorama that lies before you.

Leaving the peak retrace your steps towards the first white hut you passed earlier. Some 5m before the hut cut right on a narrow path, which drops down to the road leading to the transmitter masts, where you'll see a signboard for Sendero de los Realillos. Angle right, down the road,

which loops down the eastern flank of Los Reales, shortly passing a building next to another transmitter mast.

On reaching a hair-pin bend where the road angles very hard to the left, look for a path that goes to the right off the road just after the bend next to a pylon. The path loops downward, following the pylon line, before breaking away to the right towards the shallow ridge-line, following green and white waymarking. The path leads through a gap in a wooden-posted fence, up over more rocky terrain, then cuts back through the fence, which was badly damaged by the 2021 fire and is sometimes hard to detect. Cutting through the fence a third time, the path runs along the ridge top before passing through the fence a final time then descending to a junction. Here, angling right for 80m, you reach the **Mirador de Salvador Guerrero (1hr 35min)**.

From the mirador retrace your steps for 80m to the junction then head straight on along a clear path following a sign, 'A.R. Los Reales'. Reaching a car parking area marked **La Plazoleta Salvador Guerrero**, follow the road past the picnic area and mountain refuge of the **Área Recreativa Los Reales** and the El Refugio restaurant and bar. ◄

The restaurant has outstanding food and views.

From the refuge follow the road past a striking bronze memorial to fallen forest firefighter Carlos Martinez Haro and loop gently downhill for approximately 1.6km back to your point of departure (**2hr 30min**).

LA SIERRA BLANCA, PARQUE NACIONAL DE LA SIERRA DE LAS NIEVES

The view from Los Cuchillos towards Africa, with La Concha (1215m) top left and Pico Reales (1452m) top right (Walk 21)

At the southern tip of the Parque Nacional de La Sierra de Las Nieves, the Sierra Blanca is associated for most people with one emblematic mountain: La Concha. Wherever you are on the coast between San Pedro and Marbella, its gracious, shell-like southern face rises up like a multi-layered cake, providing a stunning backdrop to the villas that dot its lower slopes. Like the rest of the Cordillera Penibética of which it forms a part, it is predominantly composed of limestone, which has been metamorphosed into alternate strata of grey and white marble, conferring its banded aspect when seen from the south.

Behind La Concha's denuded, sea-facing slope a more verdant swathe of sierra stretches between Istán and Ojén and north and south from the Refugio de Juanar. Repopulated stands of pines and ancient groves of olives, almonds and chestnuts are interspersed with forests of holm and cork oak, along with small stands of Spanish firs. The arboreal diversity and abundance of game makes walking in the area all the more special and explains why it was a hunting reserve. It's easy to see how groups of Republicans were able to fight on against Franco, retreating from the Nationalist troops to Sierra Blanca's dense forests and deep gorges.

121

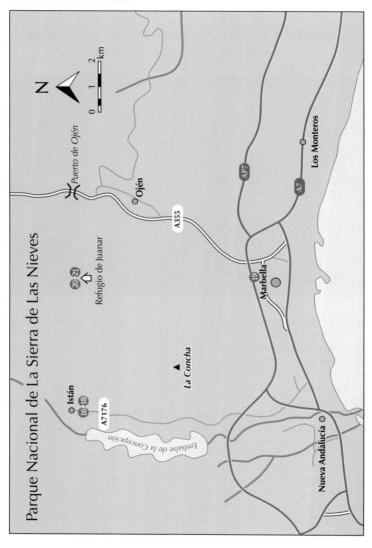

Many of the traditional resources of the sierra are no longer exploited: charcoal from its oak trees, talcum powder, marble, iron and magnesium from its mines and quarries, and esparto grass and fan palm for basket manufacture, while the groves of olives that were once worked around the Cortijo de Juanar lie abandoned. The farm has been reborn as a centre for research into the Spanish ibex (*Capra hispanica*), whose numbers have multiplied since they were declared a protected species: on any walk that passes close to Juanar (Walks 20 and 21) you'll spot them on the higher rock faces.

Other mammals present in the sierra include roe deer, foxes, badgers, genets and Egyptian mongoose. Raptors are easy to spot, the sierra being home to griffon vultures and several types of eagle, as well as to hawks, kestrels and a variety of owls.

The two villages that lie to the east and west of the Sierra Blanca feel surprisingly remote from the nearby Costa del Sol, especially Istán. This pretty white village is the start point for some of the region's most exciting trails (Walks 16–18) and a gateway to the Sierra de Las Nieves, which in 2021 was awarded Parque 'Nacional' rather than 'Natural' status. The additional kudos the title has bestowed means stricter conservation laws are being introduced, which will help protect this UNESCO Biosphere Reserve.

WHERE TO STAY

Istán has one good, small hotel just to its south and a second, very smart recently reopened one at the top end of the town above the municipal swimming pool, and is linked to Marbella by bus or an inexpensive taxi ride. Ojén is more easily reached from the coast and has a charming main square with a friendly, small hotel to one side.

No visit to this region would be complete without a stay, or at least a meal, at the Refugio de Juanar. The refuge is at the centre of the park and accessed by a serpentine mountain road. The hotel retains some of the cosy-rustic feel of the original lodge, complete with open fires in winter. The hunting trophies have been replaced with modern art. It's an exceptionally peaceful place and you'll understand why Charles de Gaulle hid away here when penning his memoirs in the early 70s. The lodge is the starting point for Walks 20 and 21. For hotel listings see Appendix B.

MAPS

All five walks in the area are covered by IGN 1:50,000 Marbella 1065 (15–45).

TAXIS

Marbella tel 952 77 44 88
Ojén tel 952 88 12 80
Istán tel 686 26 24 81

WALK 16
Istán circuit via the Infierno valley

Start/finish	The town hall (ayuntamiento) of Istán
Distance	14km
Ascent/descent	575m
Grade	Medium/Difficult
Time	4hr 20min
Refreshments	None on route, although Istan has several
Access	Istan is at the end of a no-through road that runs up from the coast near Marbella. Park up to the right, just before the main village. It is a short stroll to the start point.

This is a varied route across mountainous terrain that takes in the Cañada del Infierno, 'Hell's footpath'. The path is somewhat arduous, very narrow in parts, with lots of exposure. However, the difficulties are relatively short lived. The first section of the walk is the easiest as you cut out of the village along a restored footpath that follows the course of a Moorish *acequia* (water channel) before swinging north past the Río Molinos spring along a broad forestry track. After a couple of kilometres the road's tarmac surface becomes more-track like as you angle east towards Monda.

The return leg is quite different in flavour as you first climb the boulder-strewn course of the Infierno before heading back to Istán via a narrow footpath that contours round the western flank of the Sierra Blanca. The path is a little overgrown and you'll be glad to have a pair of long trousers or gaiters in your pack. Put time aside to visit the village's pretty central plaza, which is just 200m beyond the starting point of the walk.

The walk begins in front of the Istán *ayuntamiento* in the Plaza de Andalucía. From here head back towards Marbella then after 50m cut left up Camino del Nacimiento. At the next junction turn right then after 100m angle left at a sign, 'Paseo Violeta'. Head along a recently restored footpath which follows an ancient water channel with a wooden barrier to its left.

Passing an aviary, then the spring of El Fuente del Pobre and then a second aviary, you reach a junction. Here

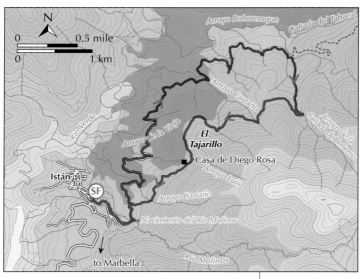

Footpath close to Istán

take the left fork and continue along the side of the water channel. Passing just above a small house with a funny little swimming pool, you reach a road, along with a large sign on the right 'Parque Natural Sierra de las Nieves'. Bear left and continue past **Nacimiento del Rio Molinos**.

> The abundant waters of **Nacimiento del Río Molinos**, which well up all year round, have been used since Arab times to irrigate the vegetable plots and groves that lie beneath Istán, channelled across the hillside via a series of *acequias*. The waters once powered a number of water mills, whence the spring's name.

Prepare yourself for a 2km-plus section of walking on tarmac as you head on north, high above the Río Verde. The tarmac becomes more track-like as the lane runs up to a fork (**1hr**). Here angle right, following a sign for Monda.

The track loops lazily round the mountain, gradually angling east and following waymarking for the GR243 Senda de la Sierra de las Nieves. Looping hard back to the left, you cross the course of the **Arroyo Castaño**. Having angled east once more and then round to the north, you pass beneath overhead power lines. After some 100m the track again swings round to the east. Passing beneath the overhead lines twice, the track descends towards a (dry) stream bed. There is a signpost warning that the path is dangerous if submerged by rainfall. A few metres before you reach it, where the track becomes concreted, cut right up the rocky stream bed of the **Arroyo de la Cañada del Infierno**. Cairns now mark your way.

At a point where a huge boulder blocks the stream, bear right and climb (hands are required) and continue up the stream bed. The path cuts past a spring-fed water tank. Following the oleander-lined stream bed for a further 400m, you reach a yellow and white PR marker post where, just ahead on a rock, you'll also see a PR 'Wrong way' cross. Here angle right, passing a second PR post, up a narrow footpath (**2hr 5min**). ◄ The path crosses an area of scree then levels as it winds along the western flank of the Sierra Blanca, back towards Istán.

Care is needed on this section: the path is narrow and at times there are steep drops to the right.

Passing a marker post, the path angles left. Climbing to a higher level, the path improves and runs on fairly level. Angling left past a rocky outcrop, it descends, crosses the (dry) stream bed of **Arroyo Castaño (2hr 45min)** then climbs as it arcs back to the right.

The path runs on through an area where olives have recently been planted and where, reaching a marker post, it angles left then right and runs on just to the left of a fence. Reaching another marker post, the path merges with a track. Here bear left, ignoring the track running downhill, then bear left again after 20m at a fork towards a metal gate. Passing right of the gate, continue along a narrow path which runs on between groves of olives. The path angles gradually left as Istán comes into view. Passing beneath the spectacular rock face of **El Tajarillo** then traversing scree, the path drops steeply down as a weird villa comes into sight down beneath you.

Cross another (dry) stream bed. Descending steeply again, the path cuts behind the **Casa de Diego Rosa** then drops down to meet with a broad dirt track. Angle left along the track through the olive groves towards Istán. Passing a farm gate and a weather vane the track loops hard right. ▶ After 40m cut left down a narrow path that zigzags down to the road. Here cut left and retrace your footsteps back to **Istán** and the Plaza de Andalucía (**4hr 20min**).

The latter section of the Cañada del Infierno

The weather vane is topped by the *Don Quixote* character Sancho Panza and his donkey.

WALK 17

Istán to the Río Verde and back

Start/finish	The town hall (*ayuntamiento*) of Istán
Distance	14.5km
Ascent/descent	570m
Grade	Medium
Time	4hr
Refreshments	Bars in Istán
Access	Istan is at the end of a no-through road that runs up from the coast near Marbella. Park up to the right, just before the main village. It is a short stroll to the start point.

This pretty walk leads north from the pretty village of Istán to the beautiful river pool of Charco del Canalón, a great spot for a dip during the summer months. The walk first leads through the irrigated terraces that lie just beyond the village: since Moorish times they have been irrigated by an intricate series of water channels (*acequias*) fed by the waters of the Río Molinos.

Angling north, you cut through a swathe of avocado plantations before ascending through the forest and then descending to the valley floor of the Río Verde. Here you follow a track along its eastern side before crossing to the west bank via stepping stones to reach Charco del Canalón. From here you can head further up the river but you'll need to wade along a water channel for a few hundred metres so this option is really only enjoyable in summer.

Set time aside at the beginning of the walk to visit Istán's diminutive main square, where there are a couple of cheap-and-cheerful bars. It all feels a thousand miles from the fast-and-frantic Costa, which is just a dozen kilometres down the road.

The walk begins in the Plaza de Andalucía next to Istán *ayuntamiento*, which you'll see on your left as you arrive from the coast. From here cut left towards the village centre, passing an esplanade with benches looking out to the Río Verde valley. Cutting right past a ceramic plaque marked Istán, you reach a three-way junction.

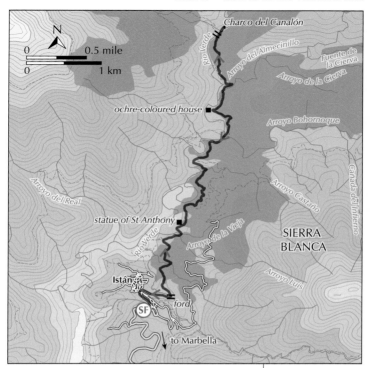

Here pass right of Bar Rincón (now closed) and to the left of the tobacco shop to drop down a flight of steps to the Unicaja bank (now closed). Here cut right again and drop down to a junction next to a children's play area.

Here, turning right, you leave the last village houses behind as you head east along a track with fences to either side. After 350m the track angles left and crosses the Arroyo de Río Molinos via a **ford**: you can cross via the concrete **footbridge** to one side. Climbing in a northerly direction, you pass a high breeze-block wall, running more or less parallel to the Río Verde, which is down to your left.

Passing the green gates of Casa Los Abuelos, the track descends then crosses a (dry) watercourse, where it angles left then climbs past a white building with twin porthole windows, daubed in graffiti. Gently descending, with great views out into the valley to your left, the track runs on through avocado groves before passing above a small white building with a **statue of Saint Anthony**. The track angles right, now running steeply uphill. The track runs under power lines high above you as views open out to the west. Reaching a point where a bigger track comes in from the right, continue straight on, now beginning to descend.

After passing through a breach in the rocks the path angles right and descends, crosses a fourth stream bed and shortly a fifth one, where you need to cut right for 15m along the rocks to pick up the continuation of the path, which shortly reaches a track on a sharp bend. Here angle right up the track then, on reaching a broader track, angle left and head down to the floor of the valley. Here follow the track north, parallel to the river's right bank.

After passing an area where cars can park then crossing the **Arroyo Bohornoque**, you reach a junction and a map of the park (**1hr 10min**). Here cut right at a sign 'Charco Canalón' up a steep concrete track then after just 10m angle left up a narrow path, which soon meets with the track again. Turn left. Climbing gently, sticking to the main track, Istán comes into view back to the south.

The track descends back towards the river, where it passes above an **ochre-coloured house**. Here the track loops right past a citrus grove, now running away from the river. After climbing steeply the track bears left and re-adopts its course parallel to the **Río Verde**. After passing above a house with a high Washingtonia palm, then another tangerine-coloured house, you reach a fork (**1hr 35min**).

Cut right, following signs for Canalón and Ruta 5 Casa El Balatín. As the track arcs left you reach another fork. Take the lower branch, which descends through pines and cork oaks to the Río Verde, which you cross via stepping stones or by slipping off your boots and wading

Damaged footbridge across the Río Verde (can be avoided!)

through. Up above you are the cables of an old **footbridge**. Beyond the river, continue up the track for 50m then cut right along a narrow path signposted Charco del Canalón.

On reaching a first fork, take the left-hand option, which crosses a (dry) stream bed. Cutting right at this point, you come to **Charco del Canalón**, which is a perfect place for a dip (**2hr**). From here retrace your steps to the car parking area and the crossing of the Arroyo Bohornoque. Continuing on the same track, now ascending, look for a track that forks right downhill with a yellow and white banded marker post. Bear right downhill and at a hairpin bend cut left on the marked path which contours around the hillside. The path is narrow and

*Rock pool on
the Río Verde*

loose underfoot. It soon reaches a dry stream gully. Enter the gully and cut right, down the bed, for about 10m to pick up the path again on the other bank. Pass across another stream bed and then through a breach in the rocks. Crossing three more stream beds, the path ascends to meet the outward track once again. From here retrace your steps to the start point. (**4hr**)

WALK 18

Istán reservoir circuit via the San Miguel chapel

Start/finish	The town hall (*ayuntamiento*) of Istán
Distance	6km
Ascent/descent	310m
Grade	Easy/Medium
Time	2hr
Refreshments	Bars in Istán
Access	Istan is at the end of a no-through road that runs up from the coast near Marbella. Park up to the right, just before the main village. It is a short stroll to the start point.

The Camino de la Cuesta would once have led down to the Río Verde, but since the building of a dam some 5km south of Istán it now leads you down to the edge of the Embalse de la Concepción reservoir. The descent is by way of a steep, stony track, which picks up the old footpath just before you reach the water's edge.

The next part of the walk is the highlight of the circuit as you follow a narrow path parallel to the water's edge before climbing steeply up to the A7176. A second steep ascent leads you past the mountain chapel of San Miguel to a higher track, which you follow back to the village. This short circuit is graded Easy/Medium rather than Easy due to the steep ascent from the reservoir.

The walk begins in the Plaza de Andalucía next to the Istán *ayuntamiento*, which you'll see on your left as you arrive from the coast. From here cut left and head in towards the village centre, passing an esplanade with benches looking out to the valley to the village's west. After passing a ceramic sign for Istán you reach a three-way junction in front of the old Bar Rincón de Curro (now closed) and the tobacco shop. Here turn left to reach a square then turn left again and exit via Calle Río. Angling right, you reach a junction where, opposite house number 20, you turn sharp left where there's a map of the walk you'll be following.

Embalse de la Concepción from Istán

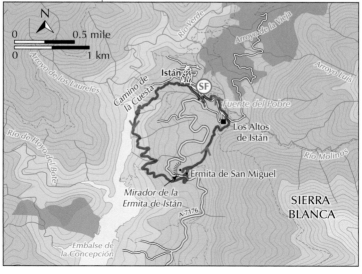

Carry straight on following a sign, '**Camino de la Cuesta**', along a concrete road that loops steeply down towards the reservoir. The steep concrete becomes a very rough track before reverting to concrete several times. At a point where the concrete track finally ends, the path deteriorates to a rain-damaged gully. On reaching a path junction by a sign facing the other way that says Atencion Vado Peligroso y Caida al Vacio, cut hard left along a more overgrown path that arcs round the edge of a gully and crosses a stream bed ▶ (**25min**) before running on parallel to the edge of the reservoir. Climbing slightly away from the water, the path enters a stand of pines then crosses a second (dry) stream bed. Still climbing steadily, the path widens to become a track, which descends and crosses another stream. Shortly, you reach a track that leads down to a house next to the reservoir (**50min**).

The path here is very narrow, loose and has a steep drop off. An alternative is to descend further to the reservoir and walk along the left hand shoreline before picking up a rising path on the left that meets with the original route once more, thus bypassing any difficulty.

Here turn left and follow the track up towards the Marbella to Istán road. ▶ Looping hard left you reach the **A7176** (**1hr 5min**). Turn left towards Istán then after

Views now open out towards the western flank of La Concha.

Terraced groves of olive and carob beneath the San Miguel chapel

30m cut right at a sign for Ermita de San Miguel. Some 25m from the road you reach a fork. Here cut right then angle left up a path to visit the **Ermita de San Miguel**. Here cut right past a signboard about La Tomillería then climb up through a terraced picnic area to a junction with a broad track.

> **La Tomillería** is a country festivity at the end of September in honour of the patron saint of Istán, San Miguel. The festival takes its name – literally 'the thyme festivity' – from the thyme that grows along the paths leading to the chapel.

Turning left, you reach the **Mirador de la Ermita de Istán**: from this high viewing platform there are vast views out to the west. From here retrace your steps back along the track and at the next junction cut left following a sign 'PRA-137 Istán' ascending a broad track that passes a number of country houses to reach the edge of the village. Here follow the track, now concreted, round to the left, passing beneath **Hotel Los Altos de Istán**. Some 20m past the hotel cut right, down a loose, stony path to a lower road.

Cut left and follow the road towards the village for 75m then branch right along a broad footpath. Sticking to the main paved path, pass a water deposit, an aviary, the **Fuente del Pobre spring** then another aviary. The path angles back to the road. Here bear right and continue down past the municipal football pitch and pool to a stop sign. Cut left then at the next junction right to return to the start point of the walk, the Plaza de Andalucía in **Istán** (**2hr**).

WALK 19

Marbella circuit via Cruz de Juanar

Start/finish	Next to the Marbella cemetery, beside the A355
Distance	13.5km
Ascent/descent	1275m
Grade	Difficult
Time	5hr 30min
Refreshments	Restaurant near the start but none en route
Access	From the A7 motorway, exit for Marbella/Ojén on the A355. Continue towards Ojén, passing two roundabouts, then turn left at a sign for Cementerio where there's parking space to your right.

Cruz de Juanar's pyramidal peak (1185m) is one of the most distinctive landmarks as you look north from the Costa del Sol. The peak is topped by a cross and a shrine to the Virgin, to which an annual pilgrimage takes place. Although this walk begins at the northern reaches of Marbella, within minutes you find yourself in wild mountain scenery. After a few kilometres of fairly level walking there's a long, steep climb up the towering Cruz de Juanar. Reaching a forestry track, a short diversion takes you to the viewpoint of the Macho Montés, from where a beautiful sandy path leads you back down to your point of departure.

With your back to the **Marbella cemetery** car park turn right along a tarmac road, following a sign for La Cascada. Just before you reach **Nueva Kaskada restaurant** cut right and climb northwards, passing a villa marked Libra, then the ramshackle buildings of Casa Marqués de Guaro. Head on past the forlorn-looking entrance to Finca Minza Manzah al Kamd, where a signboard details the route you'll be following. ▶

The tarmac surface turns to dirt as you pass a metal barrier: you'll see PR waymarking.

Passing a spring, the peak of El Juanar comes into sight as the track runs on between pine, carob and eucalyptus, parallel to the bed of the **Vertiente de la Laja**.

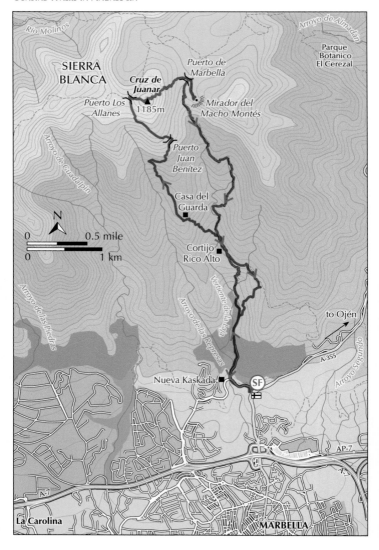

Reaching a fork and branching right, continue up a steep and stony track: rough stone steps to its right make the climb easier. Swinging left, the track reaches a white hut fed by a water pipe (**40min**). Here cut right, up a narrow, stony path that zigzags steeply upwards, cobbled in parts. ▸

Zigzagging past a hollow in the rock face, at times close to the water pipe, the path levels as it bears left through low-growing vegetation to reach the back wall of the ruined **Cortijo Rico Alto**. Passing to the right of the ruin, following a sign for Juanar, after 100m you cross a water channel then reach Puerto Rico Alto. Here continue straight ahead, following a sign 'Juanar'.

The path runs level through the pine forest before reaching another junction. Here cut left, following a sign 'Casa del Guarda', drop down and cross a (dry) stream bed, then follow a sandy footpath steeply up to the abandoned forestry post of **Casa del Guarda**, marked by a signboard (**1hr 45min**).

To your left you'll now see a spectacular overhang, a popular destination for rock climbers.

The Casa del Guarda

Heading straight past the ruin, after 150m you come to another junction. Here cut right, following a sign 'Juanar'. The path runs up towards Cruz de Juanar before angling down across the hillside then beginning to ascend once more. After angling left and passing above a steep rock face you reach a swathe of exposed rock. Angle sharply right, across the smooth surface of the rock, then continue up the narrow path, which runs up across the hillside before it enters a stand of low-growing pine and juniper.

The path now adopts a more northerly course, along the top of a ridge, before it cuts right towards a rocky outcrop. Passing through a breach in the rocks you reach the pass of **Puerto Juan Benítez**. Here cut left at a sign for La Concha along a sandy path that climbs in a northwesterly direction to a junction at the pass of **Puerto Los Allanes**. Here cut right and follow a steep path up to the peak of **Cruz de Juanar**, topped by a metal cross and a tiny oratory containing a small statue of the Virgin (**3hr 5min**).

Legend tells that a fishing boat was lost in heavy seas and dense fog when the sky miraculously opened to reveal the **Juanar peak**, thus allowing the sailors to plot a safe course back to port. In gratitude, a shrine was built to the Virgen del Carmen, the patron saint of sailors, on top of the peak.

Statue of the Virgin and Child at Cruz de Juanar

From the cross retrace your steps for a few metres then on reaching a rock daubed with paint, angle right, then right again, to pick up an indistinct path that zigzags down the eastern side of the peak. The path becomes clearer as it levels and runs across a swathe of clearer ground before entering a stand of pines. A few metres before the path runs up to a broad track you reach a sign '**Puerto de Marbella**' (**3hr 30min**).

Here continue straight ahead. Angling right along the track for 200m, you pass a first viewpoint then reach the **Mirador del Macho Montés,** from where there are vast views out across the Med' and eastwards along the Costa del Sol.

From the *mirador* head back to the wooden signpost at 3hr 30min then cut left, following a sign 'Marbella'. From here a beautiful sandy path leads down through the pine trees to reach the valley floor, where the tree cover becomes somewhat denser.

Passing a spring with a low stone wall, the path crosses a (dry) stream bed then runs on through the forest to reach the junction you passed earlier in the walk on your ascent to the Casa del Guarda. From here head back to Cortijo Rico Alto. Here, deviating from the path you followed earlier, cut left at a sign 'GR249 Ojén', along a clear path that climbs gently across the hillside.

After descending and crossing a (dry) stream the path resumes its ascent before running down once more and crossing a second stream bed before reaching a junction. Here, cutting right at a sign for Marbella, drop back down to the track you followed earlier in the day, then turn left and retrace your steps to the Marbella cemetery (**5hr 30min**).

Statue of male ibex at the Mirador del Macho Montés

WALK 20

Ascent of La Concha from Refugio de Juanar

Start/finish	Refugio de Juanar
Distance	15km
Ascent/descent	720m
Grade	Medium/Difficult
Time	5hr
Refreshments	None en route
Access	From the A7 motorway, exit for Marbella/Ojén on the A355. Continue towards Ojén via two roundabouts. Passing two turnings off right towards the village, cut left from the A355 at a sign 'Refugio de Juanar' along the MA5300, which you follow all the way to the refuge.

Marbella without La Concha (1215m) would be like Cape Town without Table Mountain. Wherever you are in the town you catch sight of its seductively symmetrical form rising volcano-like above the coast, its appearance constantly changing as the sun slips round the horizon. The views from its summit are mesmerising: east and west along the coast, south to Morocco and all the way northwest to the Sierra Nevada on a clear day.

This classic route up the mountain numbers among Andalucía's most special walking adventures. You approach the peak from its northern side, setting out from Refugio de Juanar (it's a wonderful place to overnight, see Appendix C). From here the walk leads you along a flat-bottomed valley before you climb steeply up through a pine forest towards the Cruz de Juanar.

After crossing a first col you follow a spectacular ridge for most of the way to La Concha: here you may occasionally feel safer using your hands as well as your feet. That said, so long as you have a head for heights you won't find the walk in the least bit intimidating.

The walk begins at the entrance of the car park of the **Refugio de Juanar**. From here descend 100m to a junction then turn right at a sign for two *miradores*. Looping up through the pines, you reach a parking area then pass to the left of a green metal gate. Passing several signs and

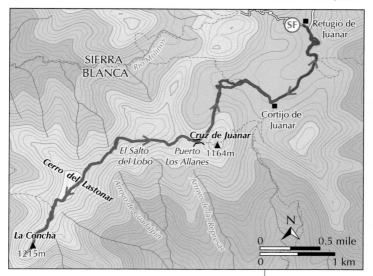

information boards, continue along the main track, following waymarking for the GR243 towards Istán. Head on along the eastern edge of a flat-bottomed valley, where an abandoned olive grove is bordered on both sides by a thick stand of pines. After passing a ruined stone hut you reach a sign for PRA-168 and a hand-painted sign, 'La Concha' (**25min**).

Here cut right, away from the track, towards the fence of **Cortijo de Juanar**, then angle hard right down through an olive grove for 100m to a four-way junction. Cutting left into a stand of pines you come to a three-way junction. Here angle left, following another sign 'PRA-168 La Concha'. The pines thin out as the path becomes sandier and climbs more steeply: you'll soon see a fence running to your left. To your left the Cruz de Juanar is visible as you climb on up the left side of the valley.

On reaching the top of the ridge and **Puerto Los Allanes**, head straight on for a few metres then angle right and continue along the ridge, heading west through

143

Olive grove and pine trees next to Cortijo de Juanar

juniper and low-growing oaks. Views now open out to the south and to the Mediterranean. Ignore a path off to the right. Having run just left of the ridge, the path cuts up right to its highest point and passes a large cairn (**1hr 25min**) before descending for several hundred metres, now just north of the ridge. ◄

Cairns as well as PR waymarking mark the way.

Angling slightly left, the path passes beneath the steep cliff face of **El Salto del Lobo**, where there are steep drops to the right: care should be taken on this section. Zigzagging steeply up left (a hands-on approach will be useful at this point) it then drops back down to a more level path, which runs on towards La Concha. ◄ As you climb back to the top of the ridge, the sea again comes into view as the path angles right, adopting a southwesterly course.

There are a couple of short chained sections along the path that will assist in showing where the path goes, as well as providing balance.

Cairns and PR waymarking still mark your path as you head on just south of the ridge before angling back up to the top of the ridge (once again you may feel safer taking an occasional hand hold) as you pass round the south side of the **Cerro del Lastonar**. A vast panorama opens out to

The summit of La Concha with the Spanish flag

the south as as you reach a cairn, where you'll see blue and red stripes on a rock. At this point you're a few metres higher (1275m) than the official summit of La Concha, at the highest point in the Sierra Blanca.

From here angle down left, following cairns and red and blue waymarking, sticking close to the ridge top. ▶ The path runs a few metres beneath the ridge, on its southern side. It is also possible and fun to walk the ridge top itself if you have a head for heights. Here carry straight on following a sign 'La Concha 15min' along the ridge to a large cairn. Here the path angles right, descends, then picks up the continuation of the ridge before climbing steeply once more.

Red and blue flashes still mark the way and lead you up to the summit of **La Concha** (**2hr 25min**). It's worth continuing along the ridge for 200m to the southern edge of La Concha to a large cairn, from where the views down to Marbella are even better. A trig point here marks 1203m. After gulping in the amazing panorama retrace your steps back to the Refugio de Juanar (**5hr**).

The Istán reservoir comes into view to the west.

145

WALK 21

Refugio de Juanar circuit via Los Cuchillos

Start/finish	Refugio de Juanar
Distance	8km
Ascent/descent	530m
Grade	Easy/Medium
Time	2hr 30min
Refreshments	None en route
Access	From the A7 motorway exit for Marbella/Ojén on the A355. Continue towards Ojén via two roundabouts. Passing two turnings off right towards the village, cut left from the A355 at a sign 'Refugio de Juanar' along the MA5300, which you follow all the way to the refuge.

This shortish, circular route takes you round the rocky massif that lies just to the north of the Refugio de Juanar, with an optional 45-minute diversion to the top of the jagged ridge of Los Cuchillos, El Picacho de Castillejos (1238m). At different stages of the walk you're treated to massive views to all four points of the compass, and the terrain through which you pass feels wild and untamed: the chances of seeing ibex are very good.

From the Puerto del Pozuelo the path to the summit of Los Cuchillos is a relatively easy climb with just a short section when you'll feel safer taking a few hand grips. Beyond the Cuchillos the path leads through a stand of pinsapo fir trees, one of the Sierra de Ojén's botanical jewels. The path is slightly overgrown in parts so slip a pair of long trousers or gaiters into your pack.

The **Refugio de Juanar** was built by the wealthy Larios family as a hunting lodge. Many an illustrious visitor was invited to hunt on the surrounding estate including King Alfonso XIII. In 1970 Charles de Gaulle hid away at Juanar when penning his memoirs. Juanar and the surrounding estate were given to the Spanish state by the Larios family in 1970.

146

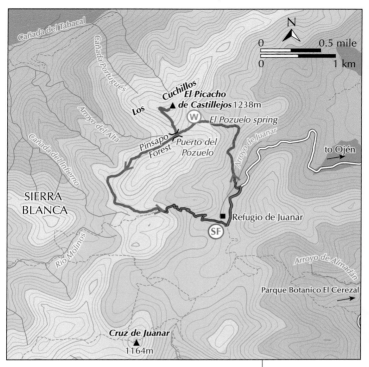

The walk begins at the entrance of the car park of the **Refugio de Juanar**. From here descend 100m to a junction then turn left along the MA5300 signposted to Málaga. Descending gently, you pass a tall, white building on the right. Before reaching a metal barrier to your left that has been clad with wood, you reach a sign for Ruta del Pozuelo (**15min**). Here cut left and follow a path which zigzags down and crosses the **Arroyo de Juanar** then climbs through low-growing Mediterranean scrub. Views open out towards the east and the north, and you shortly get your first sight of the Mediterranean before passing through a breach in a low ridge (**35min**).

147

Beyond the breach the path angles left and adopts a more westerly course: you now have a ravine to your right. As you descend, the path crosses a (dry) stream then climbs steeply before crossing back to the stream's left bank. Continue up towards the jagged ridge of Los Cuchillos. Ignoring a path off right after 100m you reach the diminutive **El Pozuelo spring**, marked by a metal sign. Here the path swings left and resumes its ascent through a swathe of more mature pines and evergreen oaks. Reaching the top of the pass, **Puerto del Pozuelo**, you arrive at a junction (**1hr 5min**).

Here cut right and follow a narrow path up through low-growing scrub. Views open out to the west towards the Sierra Bermeja. Reaching a rock field on the western side of **Los Cuchillos**, the path bears slightly left, running more or less along the top of the treeline, more overgrown and loose in parts, heading straight towards a steep rock face. Some 70m before you reach this west-facing rock face, angle right at a cairn and follow the cairns up a steep, loose path. Reaching the ridge top, the path angles right.

Heading almost due east, you reach a junction where a path drops down to the left and the eastern side of the

Footpath leading from Arroyo del Juanar to the Pozuelo spring

*View eastwards
from the summit
of El Picacho de
Castillejos (1238m)*

ridge. Don't take this path but rather head straight ahead and pick your way up across the rocks – there's no clear path but there are cairns – to reach the highest point of Los Cuchillos, **El Picacho de Castillejos (1hr 30min)**. ▶

From here retrace your steps back to the Puerto del Pozuelo (**1hr 50min**), where you should bear right in a southwesterly direction. Descending gently, the path then runs uphill once more and cuts through a stand of pinsapo pines.

Shortly, a fence runs over to your left. As you round a bluff the fence cuts up left. Here angle right then arc hard round to the left. Descending through the last of the pinsapos, you come to a flatter area. Here the path angles left as the northern flank of La Concha comes into view. Pass through a more denuded area, evidence of a recent forest fire. Passing through a breach in the rocky hillside, the path becomes sandier as it runs gently uphill to meet with a track. Here bear left and follow the stony track steeply downwards.

Cutting into the swathe of pollarded chestnut trees that surround the refuge, you pass a chain blocking vehicle access then cut right to reach the road. Angling left, you return to the start point of the walk, the Refugio de Juanar (**2hr 30min**).

The views from the peak are outstanding and make the detour very much worthwhile.

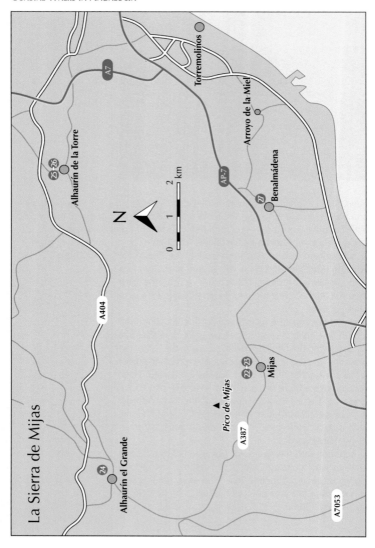

LA SIERRA DE MIJAS

Footpath through the pine forest close to Alhaurín el Grande (Walk 24)

At the southernmost tip of the Cordillera Bética the compact massif of the Sierra de Mijas rises like a defiant buttress above the resorts, golf courses and motorways of the central Costa del Sol, a green lung between the Mediterranean and the Guadalhorce valley.

The area is a Paraje Natural, which affords it much-needed protection from developers and irresponsible land owners. The mild temperatures of this part of the coast, with an average of some 3000 hours of sunshine per annum, ensure that you can walk comfortably here all year round, with the possible exception of July and August.

If proximity to the coast has meant that the sierra has long been exploited for its mineral resources, there are still wild tracts of forest and mountain to be explored, especially on its northern face. On all four sides the massif rises steeply up to 1000 metres or more, and all of the walks described in this section involve steep sections of climbing.

The network of footpaths is generally well maintained, waymarking has recently been renewed and the vegetation is surprisingly varied given its reduced surface area. If fauna is less abundant than in other parts of the coastal mountains – although you may be lucky enough to spot a genet, fox, ibex or roe deer – there are many resident raptors including imperial and booted eagles, as well as the enormous eagle owl.

Since Roman times the Sierra de Mijas has been quarried for dolomitic white marble. The stone was highly valued by the Patricians of Rome, and the proximity of the mines to the sea meant that it could be easily shipped back to the Empire's capital.

Lead, silver, iron and zinc were also all once mined while, nowadays, on the north-facing slopes, an enormous quarry above Alhaurín still works the sierra's limestone outcrops for the production of cement and plaster. The quarry has been at the centre of a long-running dispute between environmental groups and the owners and workers. There's no denying that the quarry has left a deep scar on the hillside above the village, and the walks described here give it a wide berth.

Vegetation is predominantly composed of reafforested swathes of Mediterranean pine, with pockets of oak, carob and wild olive, beneath which the predominant species are thyme, rosemary, fan palm and gorse. In the past the forests were decimated due to charcoal production, while proximity to the capital meant that they were a convenient source of wood for construction.

The dangers of the reafforestation in the last century with fast-growing pine rather than indigenous species have recently been made manifest with two major forest fires ravaging the massif's northern flank, the most recent being a 2000-hectare fire in July 2022 that required over 400 firefighters to bring it under control. At times the fire was advancing at over 50m per minute. You will see evidence of the fires most clearly on Walk 26. Earlier fires in 2001 above Mijas are barely detectable now as the vegetation has recovered so well.

WHERE TO STAY

At the southern fringe of the mountains are two of Málaga's prettiest villages, Benalmádena and Mijas, which should not be confused with the coastal settlements of the same name. The former has won accolades and prizes following its recent prettification and the village has an excellent, small *posada* (inn) in a quiet backstreet. For hotel listings see Appendix B.

MAPS

All five walks in the area are covered by IGN 1:50,000 Fuengirola 1066 (16–45).

TAXIS

Mijas tel 952 47 65 93
Benalmádena tel 952 44 15 45
Alhaurín de la Torre tel 952 41 04 44
Alhaurín el Grande tel 952 49 10 10

WALK 22

Mijas circuit via the Pico de Mijas

Start/finish	The Mirador de Mijas, above the village on the lower side of the A387
Distance	14km
Ascent/descent	850m
Grade	Medium/Difficult
Time	4hr 55min
Refreshments	None en route
Access	From the A7/E15 exit for Fuengirola/Mijas. Arriving in Mijas at a roundabout with three palm trees, turn left and at the next roundabout, take the A387 towards Coín/Alhaurín. After 1km you reach a parking area to your left, the Mirador de Mijas.

This averagely challenging walk links three of the local networks of footpaths to make a more interesting circular route. Climbing steeply from the village by way of Stations of the Cross, you pass the chapel Ermita del Calvario. From here you have a steep climb of 700m to the Pico de Mijas (1150m), which is easily recognised on the approach thanks to its meteorological receptor, known locally as La Bola.

If you plan to break for a picnic, it's worth diverting a few hundred metres to the east to the top of a slightly lower peak, which has a wilder feel and the same panoramic views. On a clear day you'll see the eastern and western Costa, Gibraltar, Málaga, the Sierra de las Nieves and the distant Sierra Nevada.

The return leg back to Mijas is longer, given that you're walking two sides of a triangle. A steep descent takes you back to a forestry track, which was created after the forest fire of 2001. From here the path runs southwest before gradually angling round towards Mijas and leading you back to the Ermita del Calvario and the walk's start point.

The walk begins at the Mirador de Mijas. With your back to the village turn right along the road. After 150m

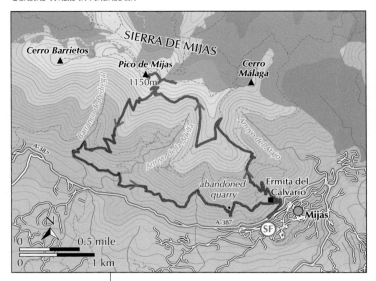

cut left up a cobbled path, passing a signboard depicting local footpaths. Followingthe Stations of the Cross upwards, you reach a junction. Cutting left, you reach the **Ermita del Calvario**.

The **Ermita del Calvario** takes its name from the Stations of the Cross, or route of the Calvary, that leads up to it from the village. The chapel was built in the early 18th century by monks of the Carmelite order as a place for retreat and contemplation. The only masses that are now celebrated here are on Fridays during Lent.

From the chapel retrace your steps for 30m then turn left and continue up a sandy path. Looping up, you reach another junction. Angle right, following a sign 'Ruta Puerto Málaga'. At the next junction angle up to the left, still following Ruta Puerto Málaga. The path zigzags steeply on up to reach a track (**45min**).

154

The Ermita del Calvario

Turn right and follow the track for 40m then cut left up the continuation of the path. Climbing on a northerly course, you reach a junction. Here angle hard left, following a sign 'Pico Mijas'. Crossing a low ridge, the path angles left then right then descends. The Pico de Mijas and La Bola come into sight. Angling right to another junction (**1hr 30min**), bear right, following another sign Pico Mijas. After running due north the path crosses a (dry) stream bed then adopts a more westerly course before crossing a second (dry) stream bed.

Shortly before the col, just east of the Pico de Mijas, you reach a junction marked by an orange-tipped way-mark post (**2hr 10min**). Here angle hard right (noting that you will later return to this point). On reaching the ridge top by a small hut, angle left along a track for 100m to a four-way junction. Some 20m before reaching the hut you can cut right along an indistinct path that leads up to another peak just to the east. It's wilder in feel than the Pico de Mijas and a great spot for a picnic.

The meteorological receptor, known as 'La Bola', at the summit of the Pico de Mijas

At the four-way junction cut left by a cairn up a steep path. On reaching a track, angle left then right to reach the **Pico de Mijas** and the meteorological observatory (**2hr 25min**). After taking in the extraordinary views retrace your steps back to the hut and head back down the path you followed earlier to the junction you passed at 2hr 10min. Here cut right, following orange waymarking along a path that descends in a southwesterly direction. Angling left, the path zigzags more steeply downwards before angling back towards Mijas.

On reaching a broad forestry track (**3hr 20min**) cut right for 25m then angle left and continue your descent of a steep footpath which, on reaching the eastern side of the **Barranco de Pedregal** stream bed, angles left and loops steeply down to a sign for Pico de Mijas. Here cut left along a broader footpath, which runs on a fairly level course before it crosses a (dry) stream bed then climbs through a stand of young pine trees and crosses a low ridge.

After crossing the (dry) stream bed of **Arroyo de la Adelfa** the path reaches a junction, where you should continue straight ahead. After crossing another ridge the path descends for some 100m to reach a wooden signpost. Here cut left, following a sign 'Ruta Cruz de la Misión'.

Reaching a stand of eucalyptus, the path begins to climb before it crosses another ridge. As the path levels you pass a signboard about *caleras* (pits where lime was made by firing limestone), beyond which you cross a ridge as views open out to the sea. After climbing once more the path descends before crossing another (dry) stream bed.

Angling right, the path runs towards a rocky outcrop then zigzags steeply down to a signpost. Cut left along a broad track, following a sign 'Ermita del Calvario' and GR249 waymarking. Reaching an **abandoned quarry**, you come to a fork. Here take the right option, passing just beneath a pylon then the quarry's graffiti-daubed rocks. The track, concreted now, climbs past another ruined building then angles right before narrowing to become a path leading to a three-way junction. Here keep straight ahead, following another sign 'Ermita del Calvario'. On reaching the chapel retrace your path to the start of the walk (**4hr 55min**).

Reaching Mijas at the end of the walk

WALK 23

Mijas circuit via Puerto Málaga

Start/finish	The Mirador de Mijas, above the village, on the lower side of the A387
Distance	11.5km
Ascent/descent	550m
Grade	Medium/Difficult
Time	3hr 15min
Refreshments	None en route
Access	From the A7/E15 exit for Fuengirola/Mijas. Arriving in Mijas at a roundabout with three palm trees, turn left and at the next roundabout take the A387 towards Coín/Alhaurín. After 1km you reach a parking area to the left, the Mirador de Mijas.

This circular walk out from Mijas could be a great introduction to the stunning mountain trails of the Sierra de Mijas. You're faced with a stiff climb early in the walk as you follow the Cañada Gertrudis up the south-facing flank of the sierra. Reaching Puerto Málaga (it's not marked on the IGN 1:50,000 map), you cross to the northern side of the range. Here you encounter a radical change in vegetation as you descend through a thick stand of oaks interspersed with pines to reach a broad forestry track, which you follow towards the east.

At this stage of the walk there are big vistas out across the Guadalhorce valley. After angling back south towards the Puerto de las Canteras you begin your descent back towards the sea. Passing the Los Arenales quarry, now disused, you pick up a narrow path that leads down to the A368. From here you're faced with a spell of road walking but within half an hour you're back at the start point of the walk.

The walk begins at the Mirador de Mijas. With your back to the village turn right along the **A387**. After 150m cut left up a cobbled path, passing a signboard depicting local footpaths and a sign for the route you'll be

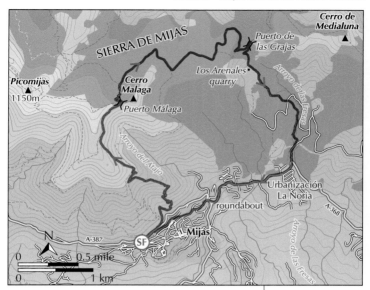

following at first, the PRA171. Following Stations of the Cross upwards, you reach a junction.

Continue straight ahead, following a sign 'Ruta Cañada Gertrudis' and yellow waymarking. Soon you cross a (dry) stream bed. The path climbs on in a northerly direction. Levelling, it swings hard left then climbs to reach a junction. Cutting right, following a sign 'Ruta Puerto Málaga', then looping steeply uphill, the path reaches a broad forestry track. Here turn right at a sign 'Ruta Puerto Málaga' then after 25m cut left up a path by a blue marker post (**50min**).

Climbing steeply towards the north, you come to another junction. Head straight ahead, following a sign 'Puerto Málaga' and a second PR sign for Puerto de las Ovejas. Climbing in an easterly direction, you reach the **Puerto Málaga pass** and a damaged information board about the *cabra montés*, the ibex (*Capra pyrenaica*) that are sometimes to be seen in this part of the sierra. ▶

Views open out towards the north.

159

Looking back to Mijas early in the walk

Passing a trig point, the path descends, at times via stone steps, through a stand of low-growing holly oaks and pines to reach a broad forestry track. Here turn right and follow the track in a northeasterly direction. Angling hard right, after 350m you reach a fork. Here head straight on along the main track, which runs on through the pines. After 1.3km the track bears right, adopting a southerly course, before it hairpins back to the left (**1hr 45min**).

Some 20m beyond a steel wire stretching between two posts (sometimes down) you reach a junction and the **Puerto de las Grajas** and a signboard marked El Pino del Puerto. Cut right along a broad track for 200m to reach another junction. Taking the left fork you descend to **Los Arenales quarry**, marked on the IGN map as Áridos. ◄ On reaching a gap in the wall 100m on past a storm drainage channel, cut left down a narrow path. Descending for some 200m, you pass above an old mine shaft. Angling left, the path, now steeper and looser underfoot, drops down to the quarry access road (**2hr 20min**).

Fuengirola and the sea come into view as a low wall runs to your left. The quarry is now landscaped, with its terraces planted with trees.

160

Here head straight on and continue down a narrow path. Descending steeply through pines, the path crosses the (dry) stream bed of the **Arroyo de las Fresas**, which it soon crosses once again, now following a disused terracotta water pipe. Passing a rocky outcrop, the path shortly angles steeply down to the left and crosses the stream bed once again. Passing left of another *calera* (lime pit), you again meet with the road you crossed earlier. Here, cutting right, you reach the **A368 (2hr 45min)**.

Turn right and prepare yourself for a spell of road walking. Passing **Urbanización La Noria**, you reach a **roundabout** and Mijas. Bear right to a second roundabout then angle left at a sign 'Centro Urbano'. Passing a line of restaurants, you come to a fork in the road. Here angle right. When you reach the village *consultorio* (doctor's surgery) cut right up Cañada Gertrudis. Follow the street round to the left then at house number 71 angle right. At the end of the street, on reaching house number 19, cut right up a flight of steps. At the first junction cut left then right once more to return to the Mirador de Mijas (**3hr 15min**).

Waymarking for the local network of footpaths

The disused quarry has now been landscaped, as required by natural park rules

WALK 24
Alhaurín el Grande circuit

Start/finish	75m beyond the BP petrol station on the east side of Alhaurín el Grande
Distance	11.5km; 14.5km
Ascent/descent	740m; 950m
Grade	Medium/Difficult; Medium/Difficult
Time	4hr; 5hr 15min
Refreshments	None en route
Access	Arriving in Alhaurín el Grande, follow the ring road to the east side of town to a roundabout with a stone cross in the middle. Cut right along Camino de Málaga. Head straight on at a roundabout next to a BP petrol station for 75m to a sign to your left marked Alhaurín el Grande, El Pueblo que yo soñé. There's parking space on either side of the sign.

This stunning half-day figure-of-eight walk is one of the most memorable in the Sierra de Mijas. The first section of the walk follows the beautiful Cañada de las Palomas, an ancient thoroughfare that climbs up towards the steep northern face of the Sierra de Mijas via the stream of the same name.

Reaching a *casa forestal* (forestry-department building), the walk takes on a different tempo as you follow a spectacular path that contours round the southern and eastern flanks of the towering massif of the Tajo del Caballo. The path at this point is one of the most precipitous in this guide. Progress will be slow and difficult at times. In 2023 there were a number of landslides that have made the path trickier underfoot. On reaching the pass of Puerto de la Encina, you have a choice.

My preferred option, which adds 3km to the route, is to continue to the summit of the Pico de Mijas (1150m). From here, on a clear day, you're treated to panoramic views that encompass the mountains of North Africa, a vast swathe of the Mediterranean Coast and range after range of the Subbaetic System. From the Encina pass another beautiful path leads back down to the *casa forestal* from where the remainder of the walk is by way of forestry tracks.

The walk begins next to a ceramic sign for Alhaurín el Grande, El Pueblo que yo soñé. Cross the road and head

along a narrow road that cuts in towards the mountains following a sign '**Cañada de las Palomas**'. Reaching a T-junction with signs 'Camino Ardalejos Chichara' pointing left and 'Camino Ardalejos Montanchez' pointing right, continue straight on up a rocky track that runs to the left of a private driveway, then continue along the old *cañada* (drovers' road and public right of way), which runs parallel to the course of a stream bed. As you climb higher the valley narrows to become a gorge.

Passing a cave, the path cuts up to a higher level before dropping back down to the stream bed, where it winds on through the rocks. Passing an old *calera* (lime pit) the path meets with a broad dirt track (**35min**). Head straight across the track and continue up the (dry) stream bed, passing from one bank to the other.

Soon the path angles left and climbs up to meet another broad track. Angle left across the track and climb a steep bank to pick up the footpath once more. On reaching a wider path, bear right and climb past a stand of cypress trees to reach a recently restored **casa forestal.** Head round to the eastern side of the building then drop down a footpath which leads down to the **Fuente del Acebuche** (**1hr 10min**).

The path below the cliffs of the Tajo del Caballo

The Fuente del Acebuche spring, close to the casa forestal

The path from the Fuente del Acebuche to the Puerto de la Encina is a serious mountain path with some challenging terrain. Parts of the path are overgrown. On the Caballo's eastern flank landslides have swept away the old drovers' path. It's passable but you will need a head for heights and some use of your hands.

Retracing your steps for 10m from the spring, you reach a point where the path divides by a carob tree. Here angle left, along a path that leads up into the pines. The path soon levels before crossing three scree slopes as you pass beneath the north-facing flank of the **Tajo del Caballo**. ◄ Angling hard right, the path runs due south, still climbing, as you cross the more denuded terrain of the Caballo's eastern side.

Angling hard to the right, you cross a scree slope before cutting back left and crossing the same scree. In 2023 landslips damaged the old path. At a point where the path appears to peter out, look for some chains on the rocks to your right. They will assist you in a short scramble above some cliffs. 50m beyond the chains the path crosses a rocky defile then angles right, descends for a short distance then climbs once more before meeting a very steep track, one of many new tracks in the area, created to assist clearing up following the 2022 fires. Head straight up the track, which soon levels a bit, shortly reaching a flat sandy area, **Puerto de la Encina (2hr 15min)**.

If you wish to climb the **Pico de Mijas** (3km up and down, requiring just over an hour and an additional height gain of 210m), head straight across this sandy clearing to pick up a footpath that angles left, fairly level at first, before climbing more steeply. The sandy path soon angles right, left, then right again before running up to a junction with a broader path at a flatter area.

Continue straight on past a cairn to reach a track. Angling left for 25m then cutting right, up a steep path, you reach the Pico de Mijas, topped by the meteorological receptor known locally as La Bola. Retrace your steps back down to Puerto de la Encina.

If you don't intend to climb the Pico de Mijas, angle right across this flat, sandy area for 15m to a marker post

The trickier section of path at Tajo del Caballo

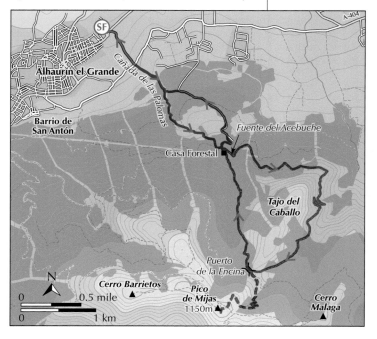

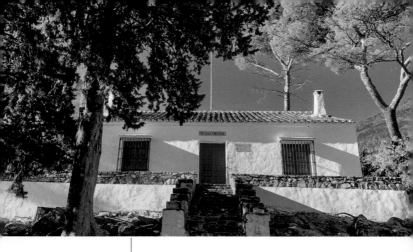

The casa forestal that is passed on the ascent and descent from Puerto de la Encina

with a blue band and a red-and-white cross, then angle right once more down a dramatic path that descends through the evergreen oaks from which the Encina pass takes its name. On cresting a low ridge and reaching a fork, take the right-hand path. Levelling out, the path cuts through the remains of an old stone wall before leading back to the *casa forestal*.

Angling left, retrace your steps back to the forestry track. Here (unless you wish to return by the same route you followed earlier) cut right down the track. Soon it bears hard left and adopts a course running back towards Alhaurín. On reaching a fork continue down the main track. ◄

Just past an abandoned olive grove the Bay of Málaga comes into view to the east.

Continue straight past two tracks, which cut left towards a house. Bearing left, you reach a junction. Here, take the right option and descend for a little over 200m. Here, as the track loops right towards two green concrete huts, cut left along an indistinct footpath which threads its way down through the pines then angles down into the stream bed to reach the Cañada de las Palomas. From here retrace your steps back to the beginning of the walk (**4hr**).

WALK 25

Alhaurín de la Torre western circuit

Start/finish	Just beyond the large, white, arched entrance to Real Sociedad de Tiro de Pichón, Alhaurín de la Torre
Distance	12.7km
Ascent/descent	440m
Grade	Medium
Time	3hr 15min
Refreshments	In Alhaurín
Access	From Alhaurín de la Torre follow signs towards Coín along the A404 (marked on some maps as the A366). Passing Venta Vázquez, continue to the km17 marker post then cut left beneath an arch marked Real Sociedad de Tiro de Pichón Jarapalo. Park on the right 50m after the archway.

This shortish circular walk leads you across the wooded hillsides of the northern flank of the Sierra de Mijas up to the solitary farmstead of Cortijo de Jarapalos, where a botanical garden has been established. It's an easy trail to follow, sticking mostly to broad forestry tracks. The early part of the walk leads you steeply up through a thick swathe of pine forest. As you climb higher a vast panorama opens before you, first to the east and the Mediterranean coastline beyond Málaga then north to the villages along the lower reaches of the Guadalhorce valley.

After climbing in a series of lazy loops you reach the terraces next to the ruined Cortijo de Jarapalos, where a number of trees, some newly planted, are marked with ceramic plates. This is a perfect place to break for a picnic, with abundant spring water and plenty of shade. After another section of track you pick up a narrow path which leads down past a water deposit, from where it's an easy ramble back to the walk's start point.

From the parking area walk up the tarmac lane to reach large metal gates at the entrance to the clay pigeon shooting club. Pass to the right of the gates, ascending a forestry track past a 'Vehicles prohibited' sign. You shortly reach a fork. Go left on the higher track, passing another 'Vehicles prohibited' sign and then immediately pass a small shrine dedicated to Juan López Perez. The track climbs through pine forest past the **Jarapalo Clay Pigeon Club**. Ignore a path off to the left signposted Urb. Pinos de Alhaurín and carry straight on. ◄ Passing a small hut you continue to climb, crossing a fire break with pylons. Ignoring a track that cuts hard left, stick to the main track, which angles right as it passes beneath a white hut with some steps.

Soon the track begins to arc back to the left and adopts a southerly course towards the northern slopes of the Sierra de Mijas. Breaking out of the pines, the track bears hard right then crosses the (dry) stream bed of **Arroyo Hondo**.

Running back northwest for some 700m, at which stage the sea beyond Málaga comes into sight, the track arcs left once more. Running on towards the south, it

As you climb higher the views open out to the north across the Guadalhorce valley.

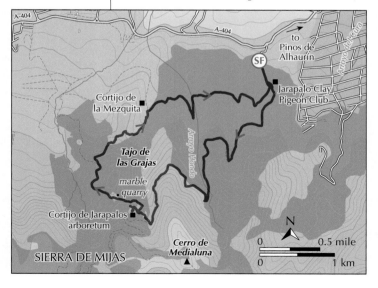

then angles right to reach a junction next to a spring (it is sometimes dry). Here take the right, lower fork, head down a track for 150m then angle left along a less distinct track (**1hr 30min**). The track ascends passing a signboard and then continuing towards **Cortijo de Jarapalos**, now fully restored. There is a small **arboretum** here with ceramic plates marking trees and plants. Spring water is channelled down across ancient terraces.

After breaking the journey retrace your steps to the junction you passed at 1hr 30min. ▶ Here angle left along the track. Reaching a divide next to a round drain cover you reach a fork. Angle left, sticking to the main track. Looping right, you pass beneath a brick construction, part of a **quarry** where marble and pyrite were once mined.

Marble has been quarried in the Sierra de Mijas since Roman times. Lead, silver, iron, agate and zinc were also once quarried here, while limestone

The view northwards from the Cortijo de Jarapalos

In July 2022 a huge forest fire covering 2000 hectares engulfed the hillsides where you are now walking. Recovery of both plants and wildlife has been remarkable, but you will see some effects of the fire as you continue.

for use in cement is still extracted from vast, open-cast mines close to Alhaurín el Grande.

The track bears gently right, adopting a course along the western flank of the **Tajo de las Grajas**. Views again open out to the north across the Guadalhorce valley. Descending, you reach a fenced compound on the left with a helipad and fire-fighting reservoir. Here take the new track on the right, which was created to clear dead forestry following the fire of 2022 (**1hr 55min**). The track contours around the hillside then descends slightly to reach a broad plateau forming part of a ridge that extends northwards. Roughly maintain your course to descend through scrubby land to pick up a narrow path that descends into the valley. The 2022 fire has made navigation trickier here; however, you will find the path is only a few metres below the plateau.

View from the path descending from the old marble quarry, showing fire damage from 2022

A stream bed runs to your right as things become more verdant. Still descending, you pass the water tank, sometimes empty, of **Cortijo de la Mezquita** (**2hr 30min**). You can't see the farm itself from here.

Descending for a little over 100m and passing through a pair of faded white gate posts you reach a broad track. Cutting right for 140m, you reach a fork. Take the right branch, following red-and-white GR marking, which leads through a second set of gate posts. The track runs on fairly level, crosses the (dry) stream bed of **Arroyo Hondo** (**2hr 50min**) then hairpins left.

Angling around to the east once more after, 250m you enter a more open area where tracks go off to the right and left. Maintain your course on the main track, still heading due east. After describing two lazy loops you return to the start point of the walk close to the shooting club of Real Sociedad de Tiro de Pichón Jarapalo (**3hr 15min**).

There are many good tapas bars in Alhaurin: this dish is berenjenas con miel *(aubergine in molasses)*

WALK 26

Alhaurín de la Torre southern circuit

Start/finish	In the southern part of Alhaurín de la Torre by a children's playground
Distance	13km
Ascent/descent	570m
Grade	Medium/Difficult
Time	4hr 15min
Refreshments	In Alhaurín
Access	Approaching from the west, head through the town along the A366. On the eastern side of the town, on reaching a large ceramic sign for Urbanización Los Manantiales, turn right up Calle Río Grande. Follow the street up past Bar Casa Paca. Head straight on at a mini-roundabout. There is a small children's playground to your right in Calle Pablo Milanés. There is ample street parking.

After a steep tarmac-lane ascent, the first section of this circular walk follows one of the most beautiful footpaths in the Sierra de Mijas, an ancient thoroughfare that connected the village of Alhaurín with those on the southern slopes of the Sierra de Mijas. The walk gathers in tempo as you climb up the Arroyo de Zambrano.

Reaching the first pass a short diversion to the east leads to the top of the Palomas peak from where you're treated to a dizzy view out across Málaga to the mountains of of Sierra de Almijara. The next section of the walk leads gradually up to a third pass, Puerto del Viento, from where you have a few kilomtres of forestry track to negotiate before picking up another lovely path leading down the Blanquillo stream.

The final section is a traverse of Alhaurín and is unavoidable due to landowner behaviour, as you will see later in the walk. The start point of the walk has changed from the first edition so as to put 1km of uphill road walk at the beginning rather than the end and get it out of the way early.

From the children's playground head up the main road, leaving the urbanisation behind. The gradient steepens as you pass some smallholdings. After around 1km, where

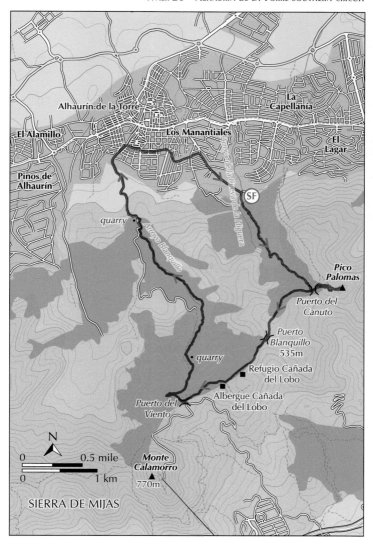

the road bears hard left, you will see a path to the right and a signboard 'GR249 Etapa Alhaurín de la Torre and Benalmádena'. From the signboard head along a broad path, in a southerly direction, parallel to a breeze-block wall, with a (dry) stream bed to your right, the **Arroyo de la Cueva de la Higuera**. Angling right, cross the (dry) stream bed and continue up through the pines parallel to the right bank. There are multiple paths here. Follow the one that runs closest to and alongside the stream bed. After 250m the path cuts back to the stream bed and crosses to its left bank.

The path runs on close to the stream, crossing from one bank to the other: the rocky defiles of the northern side of the Sierra de Mijas now tower majestically above you. Reaching a flatter area, more denuded of vegetation, the path angles left then climbs to reach the top of the pass of **Puerto del Canuto** and a junction, where a sign 'Benalmádena 9.5kms' points to the right. Here cut left along a footpath (marked by yellow dots) that runs steeply away from the col in a northeasterly direction.

After around 60m the path braids. Keep straight on up through the middle of some scrubby bushes and then

keep angling slightly right on the main path (turning left would lead you to the top of the Jabalcúzar peak) then make your way along a path which threads indistinctly through the rocks up to the graffiti-daubed trig point marking the summit of **Pico Palomas** (**1hr 5min**). ▶ The view of the coast running away to the east is breathtaking, with a great panorama of Málaga airport adding to the drama.

From the peak make your way back down to the col at Puerto del Canuto and the wooden marker post. Head straight on in a westerly direction, close to the spine of the ridge. Follow the pretty path with its red and white markers for the GR249. To your right the Alhaurín quarry comes briefly into view.

The path begins to descend, becoming looser underfoot. Climbing once more, you pass a path that cuts left as you reach **Puerto Blanquillo**. Keep straight ahead. You shortly pass another path cutting down left: again, head straight on to reach a pylon and tower that were part of an aerial lift for transporting rock from the quarry, which is down to your left. Continuing along the ridge, the path

Just to the west of the peak is a second, slightly lower peak, also marked with a trig point, this one free of graffiti: you may prefer this spot to be your vantage point.

broadens to become a track as you pass the **Refugio Cañada del Lobo**.

The track runs on, flanked by incongruous street lights, towards a fire observation tower. Passing a second building, **Albergue Cañada del Lobo**, you reach a junction with red-and-white marker posts and signs for Montes de Torremolinos and Cañada del Lobo. Here cut right. Cutting left would take you to a *mirador* just beyond the albergue, from where you're treated to more soaring views of the Costa. The track runs on parallel to the ridge top before descending to a junction at **Puerto del Viento** pass (**2hr 15min**), where it becomes concreted.

Here cut right for 10m, away from the GR marking, then turn right again past a sign 'Prohibido La Circulación de Vehículos a Motor No Autorizados'. After 25m the track divides. You can take either fork: the one to the left is a much steeper descent. After looping down, the track adopts a northerly course. Reaching a quarried area on the left, angle right and continue parallel to the track on a narrow footpath.

Leaving the **quarry**, the path drops loosely down to the (dry) stream bed of **Arroyo Blanquillo**. Things become much prettier as you follow the stream bed down towards Alhaurín; on reaching a fork, keep left. Eventually you reach a junction with an asphalted track (**3hr 15min**). Turn right and continue down towards the village. Passing the graffiti-daubed buildings of an **abandoned quarry**, you reach the first houses of the village then come to a bridge.

Beyond the bridge cut sharp right then follow a path along the northern side of the Parque Juan Pablo II. At the far end of the park continue straight on to reach a roundabout with palm trees. Head straight on past Apartamentos Santa Clara then follow the road as it angles right. After 150m you reach a junction. Cut left along Calle Peteñeras then at the next junction continue straight ahead along Calle Pablo Milanés to your start point (**4hr 15min**).

WALK 27
Benalmádena circuit

Start/finish	At the eastern end of Benalmádena, beside the A368, in front of the Centro Veterinario
Distance	8km
Ascent/descent	540m
Grade	Medium/Difficult
Time	2hr 50min
Refreshments	In Benalmádena
Access	From the A7/E15 motorway take exit 217 for Mijas/Benalmádena. Head through the top end of Benalmádena then continue along the A368 towards Arroyo de la Miel until you see a blue-fronted building to your right, the Centro Veterinario, and a signboard marking local walks to your left. There's parking both to the right and left.

Even though this walk begins close to the busy coastal motorway, just east of Benalmádena, you soon leave the rumble of traffic behind as you climb steeply away from the village. After a long ascent things get much easier as you head along a high ridge that runs east towards the Calamorro peak. The views at this stage are magnificent: on a clear day you'll see the mountains of North Africa to the southwest, as well as the mountain ranges beyond Málaga to the east. Bear in mind that the return path, which loops down in front of the spectacular cliff face of Tajo de la Sabia, is steep and loose in parts.

With your back to the Centro Veterinario at the eastern edge of Benalmádena cross the road to a map, turn right then immediately left and climb to the top of Calle Luis Cernuda. Reaching a roundabout, head straight on to a children's play area. Head straight on along a path that passes just to its left. Here you will find signboards for the GR249 Gran Sendero de Málaga and this walk. Go through a small, green metal gate just right of a marker post, drop down a flight of steps and follow a **tunnel** under the motorway. After leaving the tunnel the path shortly reaches a junction with a marker post with white

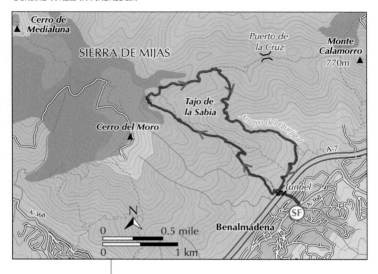

and yellow markings. Here cut hard left up to a broad plateau with two informational signboards. Here go right up a narrower path, which climbs up into an abandoned olive grove. Olives give way to pines as the path climbs steeply upwards, passing beneath power cables, parallel to a stream which is down to your right. Angling right the path cuts down to the stream bed, which you follow steeply on up.

Following a black plastic pipe, you reach a small, concreted depression, where the pipe ends. Here angle right and continue to climb steeply on up a tributary of the stream you've been following. ◄

The stream bed widens as views open out back to the sea.

After angling gradually away from the stream, the path crosses an area of scree then climbs to reach a junction where there is a pile of rocks and a signpost for the GR249. Here angle left and continue on up. Great views open out to the east towards the steep cliff face of **Tajo de la Sabia**. After arcing right through a thicker stand of pines, views open out along the coast to the mountain ranges east of Málaga. After a short downhill section the path again

Looking south towards Benalmádena Costa

climbs steeply, now stonier underfoot, to reach a junction. Here take the right-hand path, which traverses the slope along to another junction with two more informational signboards for the Sendero Tajo de la Sabia. Maintain your course, descending gently, passing a signboard about the Tajo de la Sabia on your right. Looking southwest at this point, you'll spot the path you followed earlier in the walk. The path loops down across a more open swathe of hillside, now sandier underfoot, then zigzags more steeply down to reach a junction (**1hr 35min**).

Here cut hard right, following a sign for PR-A56 Inicio Sendero and two more signboards. The path zigzags down towards the sea, shortly reaching a stream bed where it threads on down between the rocks. Angling right, the path soon adopts a course high above the stream's right bank. Angling hard to the right and climbing for a short distance towards the steep cliff face of Tajo de la Sabia, the path then arcs left once more and drops down into thicker vegetation, where it crosses a tributary of the **Arroyo del Quejigal**.

There are multiple waymarked paths in this area

Passing a junction, where to your left there's a dry spring and a signboard, the path crosses the Arroyo del Quejigal then climbs and adopts a course more or less parallel to the stream, which is now down to your left.

Passing a sentry-box-like inspection hut marked 3, the path descends more steeply and crosses a scree slope then passes a second white hut, also marked 3, beyond which it reaches a junction. Here angle right, following a sign 'Benalmádena 1km', and another sign for Ruta 4. After 75m the path passes just right of another white hut, this one daubed with graffiti. After climbing then passing a fourth hut the path runs on parallel to the motorway. On reaching a fifth white hut keep left, ignoring a sign for Ruta 4, which points up to the right.

Shortly, the path angles sharply to the right, then angles left once more. Cutting sharply right once more the path climbs for 20m then, passing another white hut, runs on parallel to a fence and the motorway. On reaching the junction where you began your climb earlier, angle left, pass back under the motorway then retrace your steps back to the walk's start point (**2hr 50min**).

3 COSTA TROPICAL

Rock pool and waterfall in the Río Chillar (Walk 32)

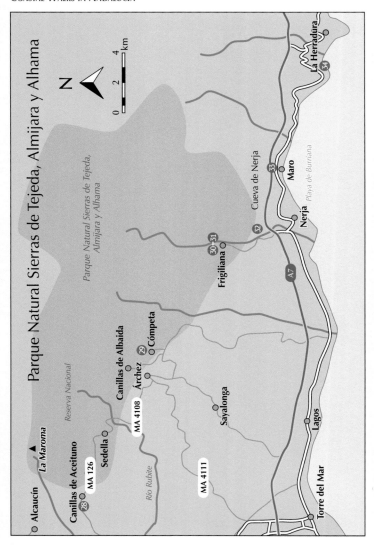

Parque Natural Sierras de Tejeda, Almijara y Alhama

PARQUE NATURAL SIERRAS DE TEJEDA, ALMIJARA Y ALHAMA

La Maroma's snowy summit looking east across the Mountains of Nerja

The Parque Natural Sierras de Tejeda, Almijara y Alhama, created in 1999, encompasses a massive 40,663-hectare slice of the Sierra Subbética and forms a natural boundary between the provinces of Granada and Málaga. The landscape of the sierra's southwestern, sea-facing flank is characterised by deep gorges and steep-sided limestone ridges, while white and grey seams of dolomitic marble give its higher reaches the look of a multi-layered cake.

Rising up behind the fertile valleys of the Costa Tropical to over 2000 metres, the towering crest of La Maroma provides a stunning backdrop to most walks in this section, especially during winter when there's sometimes snow on its higher reaches. The ascent of the peak from Canillas de Aceituno (Walk 28) numbers among Andalucía's most spectacular on-foot adventures.

The park is home to Spain's largest population of ibex. Since hunting of the mammals was limited by law in the 1970s numbers have increased 10-fold, and it's estimated that the resident population now numbers more than 2000. A similarly rapid appearance has recently been made by the red squirrel, which in just three years spread from east to west across the park. And this is a superb area for raptor spotting, with resident breeding pairs of golden and Bonelli's eagles, along with short-toed and booted eagles during the migratory season. Small numbers of peregrine falcons are also resident in the mountains.

A belt of white villages, nearly all with views down to the Mediterranean, fans out along the southern flank of the mountains, and most walks described in this section follow the old muleteer paths, many of Moorish origins, that linked these different villages. The wild terrain of La Maroma's southern flank is in marked contrast to the swathe of land between the villages and the sea, which is extensively cultivated and peppered with small farmsteads. A huge variety of subtropical species are grown including avocado, mango, pomegranate, custard fruit and lychee.

Cultivation is aided by a benign climate and an intricate system of irrigation: many of the water channels or *acequias* date back to the Moorish period. The hillsides, especially round Cómpeta, are covered with olive groves and vineyards where the sweet *Moscatel* (Muscat) grape is grown. Nearly all of the region's farms have one or more of the characteristic platforms or *secaderos*, which are used to sun-dry and fortify the grapes,

Prickly pears and avocado close to Canillas de Albaida

which are then transformed into *vino de moscatel*.

Maro, Frigiliana and Nerja had their moment of glory when land around the villages was planted with cane for sugar manufacture: the crop thrived thanks to the region's sub-tropical climate. The industry rapidly declined in the early 20th century when it proved unable to compete with sugar manufactured from beet. The ruins of a number of factories or *ingenios* are all that remain of what was once a cornerstone of the local economy.

The beauty of this area is not just on terra firma: the turquoise waters at the base of the coastal cliffs are picture-perfect and offer some of the finest scuba diving on the Mediterranean Coast, while the beaches of Cantarriján and El Cañuelo, which you'll visit if you walk the Herradura circuit described here (Walk 34), are two of the loveliest of the Costa.

Just behind Maro, at the start of the walk up to Frigiliana (Walk 33), the Cueva de Nerja should not be missed. This complex of underground caverns and lakes, complete with ancient rock art, was discovered by a group of Maro schoolboys hunting for bats in 1959. It numbers among Spain's most fascinating cave systems.

WHERE TO STAY

Frigiliana has won numerous prizes for conservation and numbers among southern Spain's prettiest villages: this would be the first choice when looking for somewhere to stay for walks at the eastern end of the mountain range. Further west Canillas de Albaida has a sleepy charm with a great little hotel plum on its main square. For hotel listings see Appendix B.

MAPS

Walks 28 and 29 are covered by IGN 1:50,000 Zafarraya 1040 (18–43), Walks 30 and 31 by Vélez Málaga 1054 (18–44), Walks 33 and 33 by Vélez Málaga 1054 (18–44) and Motril 1055 (19–44), and Walk 34 by Motril 1055 (19–44).

TAXIS

Nerja/Maro tel 952 52 05 37
Frigiliana tel 622 10 10 95

WALK 28

Ascent of La Maroma from Canillas de Aceituno

Start/finish	La Plaza de la Constitución, the main square of Canillas de Aceituno
Distance	19.5km
Ascent/descent	1675m
Grade	Difficult
Time	7hr 35min
Refreshments	None en route
Access	Arriving in the village from the west, head towards the village centre along Avenida de Andalucía then park in the village's huge multi-storey car park. Head straight into the village from here to reach the lower end of the Plaza de la Constitución.

La Maroma is a big mountain in every sense. There are numerous ascent paths, which is not that common for Spanish peaks. The routes to the top from the northern side of the massif tend to start at a higher base altitude and are therefore shorter. The Cicerone guide *The Mountains of Nerja* has four routes on this great mountain. However, of the three better-known routes leading to the summit of La Maroma (2066m), the one that departs from Canillas de Aceituno gets my vote. For most of the way up and down you have glorious views back to the Med', and the route leads past the magnificent south face of Loma de la Capellanía to the spectacular promontory of Proa del Barco (The Ship's Prow), where the views out west give a foretaste of those awaiting at the summit. The vast vistas from the summit are particularly memorable when the Sierra Nevada is cloaked in its winter mantle of snow.

After retracing your steps back to Puerto de los Charcones you follow a different path to the village, descending parallel to the gorge of Los Almanchares along the path that once was used to bring down ice from the summit. This is a tough walk; allow a full day and take plenty of food and water.

The walk begins in the main square of **Canillas de Aceituno**, La Plaza de la Constitución. Facing the town hall, exit at its top, left-hand corner then cut right past a statue with a bust and guitar, following a sign 'La Maroma'.

Angling left then right, continue up a narrow street, ignoring a sign off right for La Rábita. Head straight on at the next junction, passing to the left of an ornamental olive tree. Angling left, the road descends to a junction then arcs left. Here turn right, following a sign 'Campo de Fútbol'.

Climbing a steep concrete road, La Cuesta de los Picachos, you pass the village cemetery then a **football pitch**, where the track angles right. After 300m cut left up a narrow path. On reaching the track once again and a bird hide, turn left. After following the track in a north-westerly direction, look for cairns to both sides of the track. Here cut right up a steep path then, reaching the track once again, head straight across.

Rejoining the track, angle left then right to reach the **Mirador de Castillejo**. Follow the track to the right then, as a concreted section ends, cut left at a cairn up a path that shortly angles back to the track, which now levels as it runs on east. Passing a **forestry building**, continue for 600m to a signpost pointing left for La Maroma (**1hr 20min**).

Here cut left through the pines down a path that crosses two (dry) stream beds then climbs past an old *calera* (lime pit). Continuing up the footpath, you pass a second *calera*. After climbing up the right side of the **Barranco de las Tejas** the path begins to descend. Some 25m before you reach the bed of the *barranco* (gorge) cut right at a cairn and marker post. After running directly away from the stream for 25m the path arcs left and climbs parallel to the stream bed: the path is overgrown at this point but soon improves as it zigzags up to the **Puerto de los Charcones** pass and a sign 'Sendero SLA142' (**2hr**).

Here cut left. Running north the path crosses a tributary of the Arroyo de las Tejas, where you pass another sign for SLA142. The path zigzags steeply up past a rocky promontory as it runs west before angling back to the right. Zigzagging up north, the path again arcs west and traverses a scree slope. Passing green arrows on a

Looking east towards La Maroma from Proa del Barco

rock, you reach the promontory of **Proa del Barco** and a marker post with a cairn at its base (2hr 55min).

Here angle right. The path becomes less distinct but cairns guide you across a vast field of rock. The **Barranco de la Cueva de Don Pedro** is now down to your left. Reaching a jagged outcrop, the path angles left. Some 30m before it reaches the tail end of the *barranco* angle right, away from the path you've been following, to pick up another that leads to the summit, initially on a due easterly course. Angling back down to a (dry) stream bed continue along its course, passing just to the right of a fenced enclosure then angle right.

Care should be taken: the path now runs close to the steep southern face of the **Loma de la Capellanía**. ▸ After angling left then crossing a rise you'll see a rounded cairn at the left side of the summit ridge. Head up to the cairn, from where, passing well to the left of a high metal pole, continue up to the tower-like trig point at the summit of La Maroma (**3hr 50min**).

From here on it's a good idea to occasionally look behind you: it will make coming back down easier.

> Some 50m to the south of the trig point at the top of La Maroma is a huge pothole, the **Sima de Maroma**. In the past this was used as a store for packed ice, which was carried down the mountain via the footpath known to locals as El Camino de la Nieve. La Maroma takes its name from the thick ropes or *maromas* that were used to pull the blocks of ice from the pothole up to the surface.

Leaving the summit, make your way back down to the pass of Los Charcones (**4hr 10min**). Here cut left through a breach in the rock. Running south along the ridge, the path angles left then zigzags down and passes a (dry) spring. Running more level, the path cuts through a stand of young pines before angling right to the top of the Rávita ridge, El Collado de la Rávita. Here, angling right you pass an SLA142 marker post.

Continuing south for 300m you reach a junction. Take the right branch. The path adopts a southwesterly course, descending towards Canillas across an area more

denuded of vegetation, high above the ravine of the **Arroyo de Almanchares**. Just before the path angles hard right you reach the cave of **La Rávita** and a signboard.

> During Moorish times three sufi mystics lived in the **Cueva de la Rávita**, which is a site of pilgrimage for the small sufi community in Andalucía. Despite its name, it isn't a cave but a mine shaft that runs 70m into the mountainside. Photos taken inside the cave often display golden circles: some people attribute these 'energy spheres' to supernatural causes, others to suspended particles of dust within the cave.

Angling right, a few metres before the cave the path reaches a **spring, La Rávita,** which in summer is little more than a trickle (**6hr 30min**). Beyond the spring pass above a fenced area (where amphibians are bred) then angle left and continue down a ridge. ◄ The path eventually descends past a signboard 'Sendero Casa de la Nieve' to a track. Turn right and follow the track for 50m then cut left at a pylon between two ramshackle farm buildings to reach the first village houses. Just before reaching a sign 'Calle Sierrecilla' cut right down a zigzagging path. Passing a sign for La Rábita angle left then right down Calle Calleja. Pass beneath an arch then at the next junction cut left to return to the walk's start point (**7hr 35min**).

The more open terrain bears witness to a recent fire.

WALK 29

Cómpeta circuit via Puerto Blanquillo

Start/finish	La Plaza de la Almijara (Cómpeta's main square)
Distance	18.5km
Ascent/descent	755m
Grade	Medium/Difficult
Time	5hr 45min
Refreshments	Canillas de Albaida and Cómpeta
Access	Competa is well signed from the two main coast roads coming from Torrox and Algarrabo. Arriving below the main town it is best to park on the approaches and then walk in to the centre.

This long loop out from Cómpeta makes a wonderful day-walk and takes in a stunning slice of the Almijara Sierra. Be sure to get going early if planning to walk this route in the warmer months, and be prepared for a rigorous start to the day: from the main square in Cómpeta to Puerto Blanquillo there's a height gain of 575m. Your efforts will be amply rewarded: the approach to Blanquillo climbs through wildly beautiful terrain and once you're over the pass the landscape changes dramatically as you drop down the lush, subtropical Cueva del Melero valley.

You may encounter lorries on the section of road that leads from the quarry down to Canillas de Albaida so try to negotiate this section between 2pm and 4pm when work stops for lunch.

The walk begins in the Plaza de la Almijara in Cómpeta. Leave the square at its top, right-hand corner up Calle Carretería. Follow the street round to the right past a fountain then turn left at house number 60 and climb a flight of concreted steps. Take the higher option at any junction. On reaching a junction beneath a high wall topped by two lemon trees, turn left. Passing Bar David, you reach the Plaza del Carmen. At the far end of the square angle right up Camino de Jata, following a sign 'Campo de Fútbol'.

At the top of the street bear left by a statue of a stag to reach the road that runs around the top of the village.

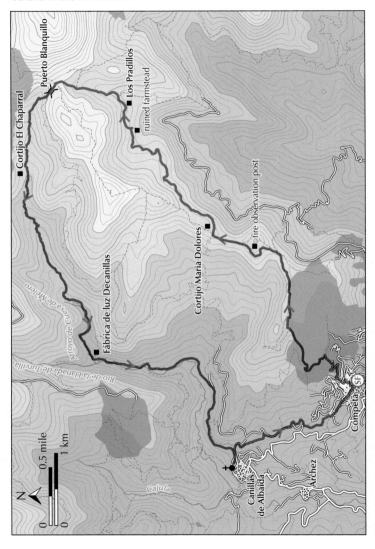

Puerto Blanquillo

Cortijo El Chaparral

Los Pradillos

ruined farmstead

fire observation post

Cortijo María Dolores

Fábrica de luz Decanillas

Arroyo de Cueva de Melero

Río de la Llanada de Turvilla

Cajula

Canillas de Albaida

Árchez

Cómpeta

N

0.5 mile

1 km

0

0

Cross the road and continue up past modern houses to the village football pitch. Just before you reach the entrance to the ground angle right then continue along a sandy path, which runs along the right side of a white wall topped with a fence. The path crosses a water pipe, passes a water deposit then angles right and reaches a broad forestry track (**35min**).

Turn left along the track, which climbs through an area denuded of trees following a forest fire. At any subsequent junctions stick to the main track, looking for GR249 waymarking. Soon, looking ahead, you'll see that the track later makes a huge loop left where you'll spot a sandy path climbing steeply away from the track. Here cut right at a cairn and more GR249 waymarking (**1hr**) along the path, which follows a line of pylons steeply upwards.

The path merges with a track which, running towards a stand of pine trees, soon levels. Up ahead you'll now see a **fire observation post** with antennae on its roof, atop a steep, convex hill. Huge views open out to the east as you continue round the base of the hill, with the hut above you to the right. Shortly, you pass the concreted road leading up to the hut. The track descends for a short distance, climbs again, then once more runs downhill. Watch carefully in case you miss it! At a point where the track arcs hard left cut right along a narrow path (**1hr 55min**).

Views out east from the path near Cortijo Maria Dolores

The path passes the abandoned farm of **Cortijo Maria Dolores** then descends. Faint red arrows and dots mark the path, which leads you past a *calera* (lime pit). Eventually, the path bears left, descends through pines, then runs past a second **ruined farmstead**. After running beside a low wall for a short distance the path climbs, passes a second *calera* then arrives at a third ruined farm, known locally as **Los Pradillos**. Here the path swings left then shortly begins to climb up the left bank of the Arroyo de Pradillos.

Keep your eyes on the left side of the path. Careful you don't miss it! At a point some 10m before the path crosses the stream bear left at a cairn, ignoring GR247 marking, then continue up the course of the stream to reach the pass of **Puerto Blanquillo (2hr 45min)**, the highest point of your walk at 1202m. Here the path runs up to a broad track.

Turn left onto the track, descending gently, and after around 250m, look for a pair of small cairns and a marker post. It's best to walk along the right-hand side of the track, looking over the edge when looking for these cairns. They are sometimes there, sometimes not. Both cairns and the post appear to fall victim to passing vehicles every so

The path to Puerto Blanquillo

often. In any event you should take the narrow zigzag path that they mark. Follow this loose sandy path, which zigzags steeply downwards. It soon improves and runs just to the left of a (dry) stream. The path shortly crosses the stream, climbs steeply, then drops down to the stream of Arroyo de la Cueva del Melero where, ahead of you is the ruined farm of **Cortijo El Chaparral**.

Don't cross the stream here but rather bear left down the left bank of the stream for 60m then cross to the opposite bank. Here the path runs parallel to a rickety fence then descends, more or less parallel to the stream's right bank. You pass through a rickety fence, its gate now collapsed. The path loops across three (dry) stream beds before reaching a bulldozed track. Here cut left down the track. After some 150m angle right along a path which soon descends back to the track, which leads you on down to the stream bed of **Arroyo de Cueva de Melero**.

Here cut right off the track along a narrow path that hugs the stream's left bank before crossing to the opposite bank. After crossing back to its left bank the path widens to become a track, which runs uphill then descends to where a metal fence soon runs to your right. Follow the fence past a water tank to a fork where, angling down to the right for 150m, you reach a gap in the fence. Cut right through the gap then angle left along a narrow path, which loops back and forth across the stream through thick stands of oleander before arriving at the **Fábrica de Luz de Canillas** (4hr 15min).

The **HEP plant**, or **Fábrica de Luz**, which supplied Canillas and other local villages with electricity, was built in 1959. It generated sufficient power from the waters of the Río Turvilla to run an olive mill and a saw mill, and to supply Canillas with its electricity. The current was prone to huge fluctuations and frequent cuts; the plant closed in 1966.

Here cross the stream a final time. Passing directly beneath the Fábrica, with the stream just metres to your right, you come to the Fábrica's car park. Head straight on down the tarmac road which hugs the left bank of the **Río de la Llanada de Turvilla**. After passing a quarry then the spring of Fuente El Chorillo the road continues down the valley to the **Chapel of San Antón (5hr 5min)**.

Climb up to the chapel for big views south towards the Med' then drop back down to the road. Here head straight ahead, following a sign for Cómpeta with a walker icon, up a steep, concreted track. Some 60m beyond a water deposit cut right at another sign for Cómpeta. The track arcs left, passes above a house with a swimming pool, then narrows to become a path, which runs between groves of olives and avocados before reaching a tarmac road.

Turn right at the road then after 300m angle left past the gate of Villa Markez and continue along a narrow footpath which cuts through a beautiful swathe of irrigated terraces. After angling left then right it broadens, now with a wooden-posted fence to its right. The path passes a builder's yard then meets with a tarmac road (Avenida de Canillas) at the outskirts of Cómpeta. Go right here, then left, and head all the way along Calle de San Antonio to return to the main square of **Cómpeta (5hr 45min)**.

The ruined farm of Cortijo El Chaparral

WALK 30
Frigiliana to El Fuerte and back

Start/finish	La Plaza del Ingenio at the entrance to Frigiliana
Distance	8.5km
Ascent/descent	730m
Grade	Medium
Time	3hr
Refreshments	None on route
Access	Frigiliana is best accessed by the road running up from the coast at Nerja. The other road coming from the north and the hills is exciting but tortuous. Park in the main town multi-storey car park, just below the centre.

Towering to almost 1000m, the rugged massif of El Fuerte provides a stunning backdrop to the pretty village of Frigiliana. The path that leads up from Frigiliana is well marked and easy to follow, even if you have some 750m of fairly steep climbing to negotiate. But the extraordinary panorama that awaits at the top more than justifies the effort.

There's a path down the mountain's southern flank that drops down to the track leading to El Acebuchal but it's steep and poorly waymarked. But returning by the same route is just as much of a treat: the vast views you get at every point along the way make this itinerary an absolute must-walk.

The walk begins in Frigiliana in the square at the entrance of the village, La Plaza del Ingenio, next to a round hut containing a puppet theatre. From here head up the cobbled road beneath El Ingenio, passing a row of ceramic plaques. Continue along Calle Real then opposite house number 9A cut right up a cobbled staircase at a sign 'Barrio Morisco-Mudéjar'. At house number 13 pass beneath an arch then bear right at a sign 'Panoramicas'.

Reaching The Garden Restaurant, the path divides. Carry on straight ahead, passing above the restaurant. After 100m the path narrows then loops steeply upwards.

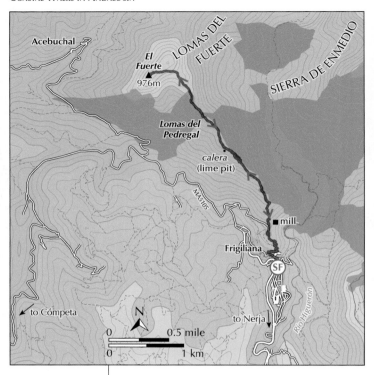

You pass several sculptures, the work of a resident British expat.

Reaching a tiled bench, head straight on following a sign 'El Castillo'. ◀

Zigzagging higher, the views open out across the village and east towards the Higuerón valley. Climbing through a swathe of young pines, you pass a dilapidated *mirador*. Passing a second *mirador*, you reach a bluff, from where you'll see a large water tank down to the left. Here cut left on a narrow path which zigzags down to a track (**15min**). Here turn right, pass the water tank then cut right up a cobbled staircase, which climbs past a **mill** then zigzags up to a pylon. Here bear left.

After climbing steeply the path angles left into a group of pines, descends for a few metres, then resumes its ascent.

The trees thin out as views open out towards the Mediterranean across the Lomas del Pedregal. The path braids quite frequently throughout this part of the ascent but they all basically meet up again. The path runs on towards the northwest, parallel to a ridge which is now to your right. Bearing right, it climbs more steeply as views briefly open out to the north. Soon the path adopts its former course to the left of the ridge before passing an old **calera** (**55min**), then runs on towards the towering massif of El Fuerte. Passing through a breach in the rocks angle left then continue to the summit of **El Fuerte** where you reach a trig point and a sign 'Fin de Sendero' (**1hr 40min**).

The Moslems that stayed on after the Reconquest (known as *Moriscos* – Moors who converted to Christianity) knew they were living on borrowed time but were loath to abandon this exquisite part of Al Andalus. Taking refuge atop the rocky

Frigiliana, the start and finish of your walk

View into the Sierra de Enmedio from the summit ridge of El Fuerte (976m)

pinnacle of **El Fuerte**, their last stand against de Zuarzo's troops in 1569 is one of the most evocative incidents of the Morisco rebellion. Some 5000 Christian soldiers defeated a slightly smaller group of Moors, of whom more than 2000 were killed in the battle or threw themselves to their death from the pinnacle's high cliffs.

Return by the same route back to the start point of the walk (**3hr**).

WALK 31

Frigiliana circuit via Cruz de Pinto

Start/finish	At the entrance to Frigiliana, La Plaza del Ingenio, next to ceramic panels
Distance	8.5km
Ascent/descent	510m
Grade	Medium
Time	3hr
Refreshments	None en route
Access	Frigiliana is best accessed by the road running up from the coast at Nerja. The other road coming from the north and the hills is exciting but tortuous. Park in the main town multi-storey car park, just below the centre.

This half-day ramble has an astonishing variety of scenery, and you're never more than 5km from Frigiliana. From the village you drop down into the spectacular gorge of the Río Higuerón. After cutting north along the river, a steep path leads up the gorge's eastern side before cutting south along the top of a ridge to the Cruz de Pinto, a hilltop shrine dedicated to La Virgen del Carmen. You then loop back down to the gorge, where you follow a path through one of its narrowest sections before climbing steeply back up to Frigiliana.

Despite the walk's relatively short mileage, don't underestimate the terrain. Some parts are steep and loose and you will likely find your walking pace slows considerably. The path through the gorge on the final section can be dangerous after heavy rain. If in doubt, having descended from the Cruz de Pinto, head across the river, climb the track that arcs up the western side of the gorge then return to the Plaza del Ingenio along the Nerja to Cómpeta road.

The walk begins in Frigiliana in the square at the entrance to the village, La Plaza del Ingenio. With your back to a series of tiled pictures head down the hill then cut left at the Unicaja bank at signs for the GR242 and GR249 and follow a concreted road steeply down to the river. Cross to its eastern bank then swing left on a broad, pebbly track. You soon pass a large water deposit, just to the left of the track, then a small white hut. Just beyond the hut

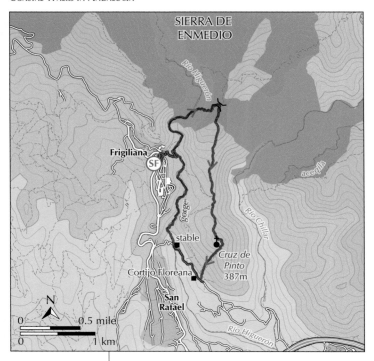

you reach a sign for Sendero Frigiliana-Fuente del Esparto. Here cut right on a narrow path, ignoring private property signage (you are allowed on the paths), climbing steeply up the side of the gorge to the top of a pass (**40min**).

Continue for a couple of metres beyond the pass and then turn right along a path that passes a GR 'wrong way' marker post with its red and white cross. Follow the narrow path marked with occasional blue dots as it ascends the ridge through an area of felled trees.

The lack of trees has afforded amazing views in all directions. The path ascends steeply to a large cairn. ◄ In the distance, you should be able to spot a pylon and, just behind it, the narrow footpath that will later lead you

Now the views open out towards the sea.

202

up to the Cruz de Pinto. The white shrine is visible on the hilltop.

Continuing from the cairn, the path descends before rising once more. It more or less follows the broad ridge top and occasionally braids. At a second large cairn keep left, on course for the pylon, and avoid being drawn too far down the hillside. Descending once more, you pass just right of a pylon. The path, broader now, angles right to a fork where a path angles left, a track right. Cut left on the path that climbs up the left side of the ridge. After a steep ascent you arrive at the **Cruz de Pinto** (**1hr 30min**).

The Higuerón Gorge

The **small shrine** of Cruz de Pinto was built in 1643 on the orders of Francisco de Pinto. He was sailing between Verona and Cádiz when a terrible storm blew up off the coast of Nerja. After he prayed to God the storm abated and his men and ships were spared. In gratitude he ordered a shrine be built overlooking the point where the miracle had taken place.

Facing the north side of the shrine, and the small black door protecting its votive offerings, cut east along

The Cruz de Pinto with El Almendrón and Cisne behind

the ridge for 40m then swing right and pick up a path that leads steeply down the hill's southern side. After descending for about 100m it passes to the left of a rocky outcrop then cuts right through a small col.

Beyond the col the path descends steeply and very loosely back into the Higuerón valley, where it reaches a track by a sign for Parque Natural. Bear left opposite a sign for Quinto Pino and descend for 200m to a junction next to a second sign for Quinto Pino. Cut sharply right up a con-creted track that climbs slightly before levelling. ◄ Soon you pass **Cortijo Floreana**. The track begins to descend, passing a number of small houses/farms and groves of olives and avocado, Cortijo El Majito, and finally a horse **stable** before it reaches the valley floor (**1hr 35min**).

A line of telegraph posts runs beside the track.

Cut right along the (dry) bed of the **Río Higuerón**. You soon pass just to the left of a red-tiled building. The indis-tinct path loops back and forth across the river and then, as the **gorge** narrows, climbs along the stream's east bank via a stone staircase, beyond which it descends steeply for a short distance. The path, cobbled in parts, passes a spring (often dry) then continues to loop back and forth across the river. You eventually reach the point where you first crossed the Higuerón at the beginning of the walk. Here cut left across the river and retrace your steps back up to your point of departure (**3hr**).

The view back north along the cleared ridge near the walk's highest point

WALK 32
Nerja circuit via the Río Chillar

Start/finish	The car park just before the barrier blocking entry to the Chillar gorge, near Nerja
Distance	15km
Ascent/descent	375m
Grade	Medium/Difficult
Time	4hr 20min
Refreshments	None en route
Access	Arriving in Nerja from Maro, head along the N-340 to a roundabout with palm trees. Turn left, following a sign 'Cahorros del Río Chillar'. Follow the road round to the right then cut left at a sign for Rastrillo into Calle Cisne. On reaching a first roundabout, turn right. Head straight over the next roundabout into Calle Mirto. On reaching a junction, turn left and follow the road down under the A7 motorway to reach a gated car park just to the right of the road. Supervised parking costs just €1 daily. If the car park is closed there's space to park a little further up the gorge.
Note	This walk should not be done after heavy rain or on a day when heavy rainfall is forecast. The water can rise suddenly.

The Chillar canyon is one of Andalucía's most spectacular natural features, a fabulous gorge that cuts a deep gash in the southern flank of the Sierra de Almijara and funnels down to little more than 2 metres at its narrowest point. It begs to be explored but this is no normal hiking trail: even during the Andalusian summer you're obliged to wade from bank to bank as you follow the river northwards, scrambling across boulders, ducking beneath tree trunks and climbing a series of waterfalls that feed several idyllic rock pools.

As this guide goes to press the path that leads along the water channel to the mill race above the HEP plant has been blocked, although there are moves afoot to reopen it. If you have a head for heights it's worth climbing up from the Río Chillar to the point where you join the channel to see if the path is now open. If it remains closed you'll need to return the way you came.

This is a well-known walk so is best tackled on a weekday. Consider taking plastic sandals or trainers for the sections of river walking.

From the **car park** head north along the river, following a track that runs past a **barrier** next to a sign 'Parque Natural Sierra Tejeda, Almijara y Alhama', beyond which you pass an area where quarrying has taken place. Crossing from one side of the **Río Chillar** to the other, you pass a group of **HEP buildings** and a sluice gate (**25min**) where, beyond a grove of eucalyptus, the gorge narrows down: from this point on you'll be wading in sections.

The gorge narrows to just arms' width (**55min**) beyond which you reach the first rock pools. The gorge widens once more as you head on up the river: you'll

The narrowest point of the Chillar gorge

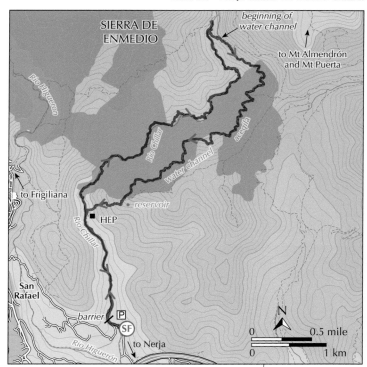

need to climb across tree trunks and scramble across boulders as you climb past a series of waterfalls with cliffs towering high above you.

Faint blue dots now mark your path as it threads gradually up through the rocks. Reaching a point where the valley has widened further still, the river braids into a series of streams. Here plot a course along the river's right bank, being prepared to use hands as well as feet. You soon reach more fabulous rock pools, one fed by a three-metre high waterfall (**1hr 50min**). ▸

This could be a point to turn back if you prefer an easier up-and-down walk.

Continue up the river bed, which adopts a northwesterly course, still marked with blue dots. The path becomes

207

clearer as it threads its way on up the river bed, between oleander, pines and lentiscus, crossing from bank to bank. You'll need to use your hands occasionally as you clamber over boulders and up low waterfalls. At a point where the path angles to the left side of the river you begin to see marker posts and more blue dots before you reach a red-and-white GR marker post pointing left (**2hr 25min**).

See introduction for this walk. Access along the path beside the water channel may remain closed. In this case you'll need to retrace your steps from here, or the point you reach the water channel, back to the beginning of the walk.

Here a path cuts up the west side of the gorge, leading to Frigiliana. Ignoring this path, retrace your steps down the gorge for some 150m, looking for red-and-white GR painted stripes. On reaching a GR249 post, angle left across the stream bed then, after following a sandy path down through the rocks, angle left again at a marker post, away from the river, along a path that loops steeply upwards. ◄ Some 350m from the river, 5m beyond another GR249 post, you reach a junction, where a broad path – in fact it's a water channel – crosses yours.

Outcrop next to the water channel above the Chillar gorge

Cut right along the **water channel**. Passing through a breach in the rocks, drop down a flight of steps then follow a fenced walkway, which leads round a rocky outcrop before passing a sluice gate (**2hr 45min**). Bearing right, the channel crosses a (dry) stream bed then passes through another breach in the rock, where the path again becomes fenced. The water channel winds on around the side of the gorge and eventually leads you to a small **reservoir** feeding a black turbine pipe (**3hr 40min**).

Heading straight on past the reservoir, you pick up a narrow footpath which loops steeply down to the left of the turbine pipe. It's steep and loose in sections. On reaching a pylon at the back of the HEP buildings you passed on your way up the gorge, cut left along a narrow footpath. Ignoring a first path that cuts steeply down to the right, continue down an overgrown, narrow path to reach the bed of the Chillar then retrace your steps back to the car park (**4hr 20min**).

The verdant section of the upper river

The water channel needs some agility and a head for heights

WALK 33
Maro to Frigiliana

Start	The entrance to the Cueva de Nerja, on the north side of Maro
Finish	Plaza del Ingenio, Frigiliana
Distance	14.5km
Ascent	930m
Descent	660m
Grade	Medium/Difficult
Time	5hr 10min
Refreshments	None en route
Access	There are regular buses between Frigiliana and Nerja but you'll then need to take a taxi up to the Nerja cave. The best option might be to leave a car in Frigiliana then take a taxi to the Cueva de Nerja: it's just a €20 fare.

This mountain trail, known to locals as El Camino del Imán, numbers among Andalucía's most spectacular walks. The trail begins in gentle mode as it heads along a broad forestry track then a shaded river bed, which lead inland from the Cueva de Nerja. On reaching the picnic area of El Pinarillo, things take on a different tempo as the trail rollercoasters its way west to Frigiliana via four deep gorges. It scarcely seems possible that such wild mountain scenery is just a few kilometres from the urban sprawl of the coast.

A large section of the route coincides with the GR249 footpath and new waymarking makes this an easy trail to follow.

The walk begins next to the green entrance gates to the **Cueva de Nerja**.

The **Cueva de Nerja**, a system of caverns that stretches for some 5km, was discovered in 1959 by a group of schoolboys who were hunting bats. One of the caverns forms a natural amphitheatre with astonishing acoustics, where concerts and dance events are held during the summer months. Entrance fee €9; for opening times see **www.cuevadenerja.es**

With your back to the gates turn right. You immediately pass signs for Fuente del Esparto and Área Recreativa El Pinarillo. After a few yards you pass a green barrier. Ignore a track that branches left but rather head straight along a broad forestry track which, climbs gradually upwards.

map continues on page 213

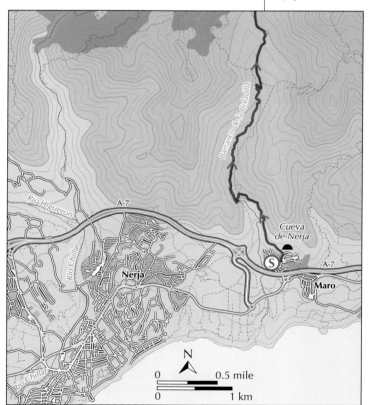

Ascent from
El Pinarillo

From here you'll be
following GR249
waymarking all the
way to Frigiliana.

After 15min, at a point where the track bears right where you'll see a GR249 post to the left of the track, cut left into the trees on a narrow path that twists its way through the undergrowth to a steep bank above the river bed of the **Barranco de la Coladilla**. Make your way carefully down the bank then angle right up the river bed. On reaching a point marked by cairns, cut right then angle back left up a stony track, which climbs out of the gorge back to the track you left earlier. Turn left along the track and continue your ascent to **El Pinarillo picnic area**. ◄

Angle left through the picnic area, passing a map of the park, a tap and a line of barbecues. After passing a threshing platform continue past a green barrier then drop down and cross a (dry) river bed. 20m beyond the river the track divides. Take the narrower, left-hand path, which climbs steeply and shortly crosses the track that you've just left.

Head on up a deeply eroded path to a broader track where, turning left and climbing, you reach the top of a **pass**, where magnificent views open out to the north and west. Here the track arcs right and runs up to a chain across the track (**2hr 15min**).

Continue past the chain for approximately 900m to a cairn and marker post. Here cut left down a narrow path which zigzags steeply down into the Chillar gorge. The path passes a small ruin and crosses a **water channel**, before descending to the river bed of the **Río Chillar (2hr 30min)**. Bear right along the river's east bank for 30m then cross to the opposite bank by way of stepping stones.

After running close to the river's west bank the path angles left and climbs away from the Chillar to a fork by a marker post. Take the left ascending fork, and avoid the right fork along the water channel (acequia), follow the path on up to the top of a second steep **pass (3hr 5min)**.

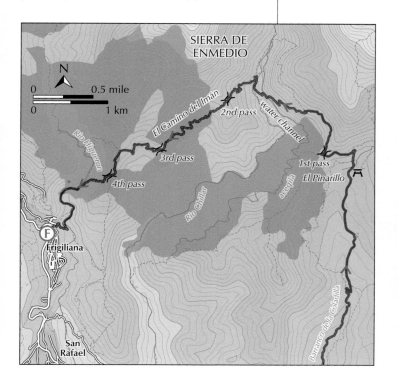

Descending into the next valley, the path crosses a (dry) stream bed and climbs for a short distance before descending once more. Crossing three more (dry) stream beds, it leads to the top of a third **pass**. As you descend into the next valley the vegetation becomes much sparser. The path again descends and crosses another (dry) stream bed before climbing to the top of the fourth and final **pass**, from where the Higuerón valley is now visible to the west. The path runs along the spine of the ridge then runs gently downhill just east of the ridge to reach a fork by a marker post (**4hr 15min**).

Here cut right, down a narrow path, which leads down through pine forest to the valley floor of the **Río Higuerón**. On reaching a sign for Frigiliana-Fuente del Esparto, angle left along the valley floor past a white hut then a large **water tank**. The track soon angles across to the river's west bank where it becomes concreted. Following the track steeply upwards through groves of avocados, you reach the Unicaja bank and, just beyond, the Plaza del Ingenio at the entrance to **Frigiliana** (**5hr 10min**). ◄

The taxi rank and bus stop are just beneath the square.

Looking back into the Chillar Gorge

WALK 34

La Herradura circuit via Cantarriján beach

Start/finish	The Mirador de Cerro Gordo and Atrévete restaurant, at the edge of La Herradura
Distance	11km
Ascent/descent	550m
Grade	Medium/Difficult
Time	3hr 30min
Refreshments	Cantarriján beach
Access	From the A7-E15 motorway exit for La Herradura/Almuñecar. On reaching a roundabout at the bottom of the hill, turn right on the N-340A towards Maro then turn right again at km305 for Cerro Gordo. Continue along the old coastal road to a sign for Mirador de Cerro Gordo. There's room to park on the left.

This figure-of-eight walk takes you past two coastal watchtowers and two of the best sweeps of sand on the Costa Tropical: Cantarriján and the mesmerisingly beautiful beach of El Cañuelo. Both beaches restrict vehicle access in summer meaning that even then you can stake a claim on the sand, and the snorkelling and diving here is among the best on the Costa.

The middle section of the walk takes you along the spine of the Caleta ridge: this is walking at its dramatic best but not for anyone who suffers from vertigo. The path on this section is less clear but waymarking and cairns help guide your way and the views from the Caleta's summit are breathtaking.

The walk entails two stretches of road walking and three steep ascents. Don't let these short sections of tarmac put you off: there's precious little traffic on the old coastal road and the views are stunning.

The walk begins next to the **Mirador de Cerro Gordo** and the Atrévete restaurant. From here follow a narrow path that passes just to the left of the restaurant. On reaching a junction signed Torre Vigia to the left and Mirador to the right, angle left to reach the **watchtower**. ▸

After visiting the tower return to the junction then turn left to reach a second *mirador* and a signboard about

The watchtower is one of many along the Andalusian seaboard that were constructed in the 17th and 18th centuries to defend it from North African pirates.

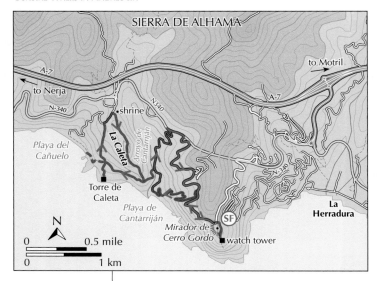

how the cliffs of this part of the coast were formed. From here return to the finger sign at the junction and turn left to retrace your steps back to the start point. Here turn left (20min) and follow a tarmac road past Casa Lupo y Lupita to a sign on the right indicating Granada in one direction and Málaga in the other. Here cut hard left past a No entry sign and another 'Paraje Natural'.

After cutting beneath a dilapidated building the road angles right then passes a number of houses then a red- and-white barrier, before descending very steeply to reach **Playa de Cantarriján (50min)**. Turn right and head along the beach past two restaurants, the second of which, Bola Marina, is arguably one of the best in Andalucía. Then cut right at an electric pole past a small bus shelter and continue up a track that runs to the left of the restaurant car parks.

After 50m angle left, away from the track, and continue up the (dry) bed of the **Arroyo de Cantarriján** for 400m, where you'll see two boulders flanking a path that cuts up to the road. Ignoring this path, angle hard left at GR paint flashes and leave the stream bed via a path that loops steeply upwards then runs towards the sea. At the top of a bluff you reach a junction (**1hr 5min**) where a path cuts up to the right. Take the left option, maintaining your course. ▸ The path braids somewhat. You will see small lines of rocks across some path spurs. These are Spanish rambler code, informing you that the spur is a dead end. Eventually, you reach a T junction.

Soon a watchtower comes into view: to your right is the towering southern face of Cerro Caleta.

Here cut left for 200m to the **Torre de Caleta**. The path twists inland briefly and ascends before reaching the tower. After visiting the tower retrace your steps back to the fork. Turning left after 40m you reach another junction.

If visiting the beach at El Cañuelo, cut left (add an extra 30min to the walk). The path runs close to the edge of a *barranco* and descends steeply through the pines before cutting right at a small cairn and angling down towards a ruin on a bluff above a tiny cove. Some 40m before the ruin angle right across the hillside along a narrow path, on a northerly course. Cutting through thick vegetation, the path drops steeply down to **Playa del Cañuelo**. Return the same way.

Looking down to Playa de Cantarriján from the path to Torre de Caleta

Here angle right, up a steep path, leaving the GR red-and-white markers and passing a red-and-white cross on a boulder. The path soon passes to the left of a ruin, crossing its old threshing floor, then climbs directly north past a second ruin before merging with a track that leads you to the access track to El Cañuelo beach. After climbing steeply the track levels. Here look carefully to the right for a white **shrine** topped by a cross.

Cut right to the shrine (dedicated to San Judas Tadeo) then angle right in front of the shrine and pick up a narrow path, which climbs steeply through the scrub and soon adopts a course along the spine of La Caleta ridge. Following cairns and blue dots, you pass a saddle before reaching the highest point on the ridge (**2hr 35min**).

Head down on the same course, on a steep loose path just left of the ridge (there are steep drops on its sea-facing side), following cairns and blue dots. After cutting through thicker undergrowth you return to the path you followed earlier in the walk (**3hr**). Turn left and retrace the path back down into the **Arroyo de Cantarriján**. Angling left between two boulders, you reach the access track to Cantarriján. Follow this steep track up to the N-340 and a barrier and car park. Turn right then after 200m branch right again at a sign 'Cerro Gordo'. Follow this quiet road back to the start point of the walk (**3hr 30min**).

4 COSTA DE ALMERÍA

The Castillo de San Ramón and Playa El Playazo (Walk 39)

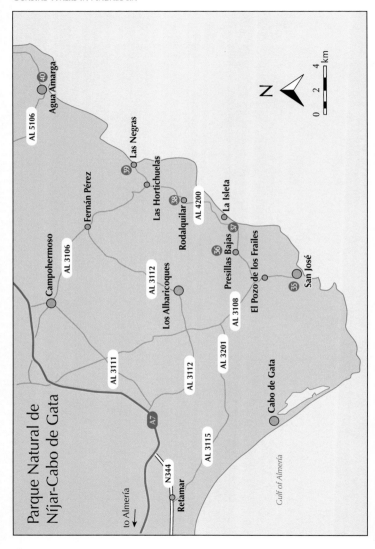

Parque Natural de
Níjar-Cabo de Gata

PARQUE NATURAL DE NÍJAR-CABO DE GATA

Deserted cala beyond Monsul (Walk 35)

The Parque Natural de Cabo de Gata is the most easterly of Andalucía's protected areas and its desert-like landscapes are hugely different to those of the other parks described in this book. This is one of the most arid areas in Europe with an average annual rainfall of less than 200 millimetres and an average annual temperature approaching 20°C. The region's warm and dry climate, together with its unusual volcanic geology, have given rise to some of the most distinctive landscapes in the Iberian peninsula.

The Phoenicians were the first to establish trading posts in the region, while during the Roman period the sheltered bays of its seaboard served as anchorage points for ships sailing between Italy and the ports of western Andalucía. Few settlements were established due to the scarcity of surface water until the arrival of the Moors, who were able to tap the region's subterranean aquifers using water wheels like those they'd left behind in North Africa.

During the Reconquest the area suffered from being a buffer zone between Islamic and Christian Spain, while after the departure of the Moors it became an uninhabited

221

backwater, unable to protect itself from the raids of North African pirates. It wasn't until the 18th century and the reign of Charles III, and the completion of a line of coastal watchtowers, that the threat of piracy disappeared and settlers from other regions of Spain began to establish fishing communities and to farm the coastal hinterland.

During the 19th century Cabo de Gata's volcanic geology briefly offered it a role on the national stage at a time when iron ore and gold were mined and refined in the area close to Rodalquilar. But greater wealth would come from open-cast andesite mining for cobblestones at a time when the streets of the largest cities in Spain were made of stones hewn from the solidified magmas of Cabo de Gata. And it was a mineral that gave the region its name: the region was once known as Cabo de Agate, or the Cape of Agate, due to the abundance of the stone in its volcanic rock. With time the name became shortened to Cabo de Gata.

The Parque Natural de Cabo de Gata was created in 1987 and encompasses a 48,500-hectare slice of the province of Almería and includes 12,000 hectares of marine reserve: its waters are home to one of Europe's best-preserved reef systems, and submarine tourism attracts divers from all over the world. The park was given additional kudos when in 1997 it was declared a UNESCO Biosphere Reserve.

The seaboard of the park escaped the unbridled development that took place along other parts of the coast due to its isolation and lack of infrastructure: by the time developers became interested in the area, they'd missed the boat. Thanks to its protected status the park is home to some of Spain's most pristine beaches and coves, while the coastal footpath that runs across the park numbers among Spain's best-kept walking secrets. The beaches that lie within the park get busy from mid June to mid September but at other times of year they're all but deserted.

The abundance of volcanic soils coupled with the region's warm, arid climate – most water remains deep underground – have given rise to unique, drought-adapted plants, which include several different xerophytes. On any walk in the park you'll see fan palm, oleander, rosemary, thyme and wild olives, as well as the occasional sculptural *Agave americana* which, as the name implies, was brought back from the New World and which has flourished in conditions similar to those of its native America.

Over 1000 plant species have been catalogued, and the park is especially beautiful in early spring when the dark slopes of its volcanic massifs take on a light-green hue and when wildflowers line the courses of its dry river beds, or *ramblas*. At other times of year the park has a haunting, mineral beauty that's evocative of the landscapes of the southern US and Mexico. It was for just this reason that the area has often been used for filming desert shoots within Europe. Sergio Leone and Clint Eastwood made their spaghetti westerns here, while several other screen classics, including *Exodus, Cleopatra, Lawrence of Arabia* and *Indiana Jones and the Last Crusade*, were filmed in the empty, dream-like landscapes that are so much a part of Cabo de Gata.

With a population density of fewer than 20 inhabitants per km^2 and with just a dozen towns and villages, there's little in the way of light pollution: night skies within the park, which is nearly always free of clouds, are simply magical.

The down side to the park's location, at the eastern end of Andalucía, is that it is in the eye of the winds that blow in hard from the east; Cabo de Gata sees an average of 300 windy days per year. But if you're hiking in hotter weather these same winds are a help rather than a hindrance, and you won't regret the leap of faith that led you to this magical corner of Iberia.

WHERE TO STAY

The area in and around Rodalquilar would make an excellent base for a walking holiday, within easy driving range of the start points of all the walks in this section. The village is about 3km back from the sea. If you prefer a seaside location, Las Negras and Agua Amarga have a wide range of accommodation, as does San José at the western end of the park. For hotel listings see Appendix B.

MAPS

Walks 35, 36 and 37 are covered by IGN 1:50,000 El Pozo de los Frailes 1060 (24–44) , Walk 38 by Pozo de los Frailes 1060 (24–44) and Carboneras 1046 (24–43), and Walks 39 and 40 by Carboneras 1046 (24–43).

TAXIS

Rodalquilar tel 671 24 40 65 or 636 79 11 27
Los Escullos/San José tel 608 05 62 55

WALK 35

San José circuit via Monsul and Los Genoveses

Start/finish	The roundabout on the southern side of San José
Distance	11.5km
Ascent/descent	335m
Grade	Medium
Time	3hr 30min
Refreshments	None en route
Access	Arriving in San José from the north, follow signs for Los Genoveses and Monsul. On reaching a roundabout at the southern side of the village where a sign points left for Guardia Civil, park to the left or right.

The beaches of Monsul and Los Genoveses number among the finest in southern Spain, and this circular walk leads you past stretches of sand, as well as looping in and out of the lesser-known Calas del Barronal.

The walk begins in gentle fashion as you follow an agave-lined path down towards the crystalline waters of Los Genoveses. Shortly before reaching the beach the path angles inland before crossing a low rise to reach Monsul. From here the path becomes less distinct as you drop in and out of a series of sandy coves before crossing a final ridge to arrive back at Los Genoveses, where a short diversion leads to the top of the headland of Morrón de los Genoveses. From here you follow the ocean's edge to the far end of the beach then retrace your steps back to San José. The section of beach walking is not possible at high tide. Check www.tide-forecast.com before you set out. The Calas (coves) del Barronal are also impassable at high tide.

From the roundabout at the south end of San José head along a broad track, following a sign 'Playa de los Genoveses/Playa de Monsul'. The track soon passes beneath a **windmill**. A few metres beyond, at the brow of a hill, cut left at a sign 'Sendero Los Genoveses' along a broad path that heads towards the sea through stands of old and damaged agave. Keeping straight ahead at any junctions and ignoring a broad pine-lined track to the left, follow the path as it leads closer to Playa de Los

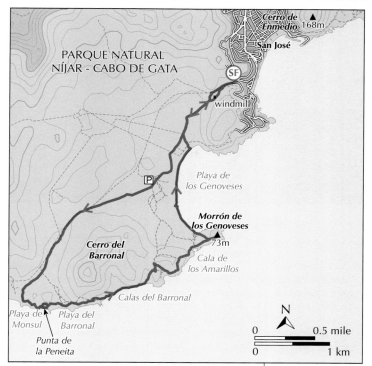

Genoveses, where you reach a low wooden fence. Here angle right, passing an old pillbox with graffiti, then continue along a sandy path that passes beneath a **car park**.

Reaching a signboard for Playa de los Genoveses, head straight ahead and continue across the coastal plain towards two buildings daubed with graffiti. The path passes well to their right. There is another larger graffiti-daubed building visible off to the right. The path is marked with marker posts with blue and white stripes. After angling right then left, the path passes beneath a power line.

On reaching a broad track and a sign 'Fin de Senda Cicable', continue along a narrow path that runs just to the

The Calas de Barronal: it is this section that can not be walked at high tide

Playa de Monsul was used as a location for the Hollywood blockbuster *Indiana Jones and the Last Crusade*. In this scene Harrison Ford and Sean Connery defeat an attacking Messerschmitt 109 with the aid of an umbrella and a flock of seagulls.

track's left. Angling away from the track, the path runs past two huts then, passing between twin metal posts, passes two more huts, the first with a projecting water pipe.

Reaching the eastern end of the **Playa de Monsul**, angle left towards a huge rock. Some 50m before the rock angle left again and climb to the highest point of a sandy bank where, angling right, you pick up an indistinct path marked with sporadic, faded blue and white way-marking, which leads up to the **Punta de la Peneita (1hr 25min)**. ◄ Here the path becomes clearer as it angles left before dropping down to a first beautiful *cala*.

From the sandy cove cut left at a huge, pockmarked, rocky outcrop and climb away from the beach for 20m then angle right along a clearer path, marked with faded waymarking and cairns. Crossing another rise, the path angles down to the **Playa del Barronal**. Continue through the dunes to the east end of the beach. Here angle left up a sandy bank then continue on the same course through a jumble of black volcanic rocks, looking for cairns.

The path becomes clearer as it angles right below a rocky summit then passes above a steep cliff face. The path here is airy and subject to continuing erosion. You will need to use hands as well as feet on some sections. A less precipitous route passes to the left of the previously mentioned rocky summit with slightly more ascent. Crossing the next headland, the path angles right then, descending indistinctly across an outcrop of volcanic rock, descends to the first beach of the **Calas del Barronal**.

Passing to the right of a fragmented outcrop of volcanic lava, whose vertical layers of rock are strangely reminiscent of one of the fallen Twin Towers in New York, you reach a second *cala*. At its far end, sticking close to the sea, you reach a third *cala* with a huge sand dune at its western end and a scree slope at its eastern edge. Here, angling 45 degrees inland, continue along the dry bed of a *rambla*.

Around 100m along the *rambla*, angle right to climb a steep path that loops up to a ridge where, angling left and inland for some 100m, the path cuts hard right before descending towards the next *cala*. Passing behind the *cala* the path climbs steeply away from the sea to the top of the next ridge, where views open out to the east and to the trig point atop Morrón de los Genoveses.

Angling left, the path climbs across a smooth rock face to reach a jagged ridge top where the Playa de los Genoveses comes into view. Angling down to the right across the hillside, the path passes to the left of **Cala de los Amarillos** then climbs steeply to the top of the **Morrón de los Genoveses** (2hr 45min).

Cala de los Amarillos

Playa de los Genoveses from the trig point at Morrón

Playa de los Genoveses takes its name from a Genovese fleet of 200 ships that was anchored in the bay in 1147 for two months while waiting to attack the Moorish settlement in Almería. In 1567 the Spanish Armada gathered in the bay in the period leading up to the Battle of Lepanto, which would end the hegemony of the Ottoman Empire in the Mediterranean.

From here retrace your steps to the base of the promontory then cut right and follow the ocean to the far end of **Los Genoveses**. Some 200m beyond a white hut, which you'll spot just to the left of the beach, cut away from the sea to reach a metal sign (it faces away from you) for Playa de los Genoveses. From here head inland along a track lined with pines to reach the footpath you followed earlier. Turn right and retrace your steps back to the beginning of the walk. It's worth cutting right just before you reach the roundabout to visit the windmill you passed earlier in the day (**3hr 30min**).

WALK 36

Presillas Bajas to Majada Redonda and back

Start/finish	The car park at the entrance to the hamlet of Presillas Bajas, at a sign 'Sendero Majada Redonda'
Distance	7km
Ascent/descent	275m
Grade	Easy
Time	1hr 50min
Refreshments	None en route
Access	From El Pozo de los Frailes take the AL3201 then the AL4200 towards Rodalquilar. Just past the km3 post turn left, following a sign 'Caldera de Majada Redonda'. Arriving in Presillas Bajas, turn left at a line of recycling bins then park to one side of the hamlet's old threshing floor.

This short, there-and-back walk could make a great first or last-day ramble when you visit the Cabo de Gata park.

Leaving the sleepy hamlet of Presillas Bajas, you head inland along the shingly bed of a *rambla* lined with palm, thyme and fig trees along with some agave: it's easy to see why this part of the park has often been used for filming westerns.

Passing the ruined farm of Los Berengueles, the path loops sharply east and into the midst of the vast crater of Majada Redonda, where you can contemplate one of the park's most striking volcanic landscapes. The abandoned terraces within the crater bear witness to the fact that less than a century ago farmers were still eking out a precarious living here: the high walls of the volcano acted as a funnel, channelling the occasional rains down to a patchwork of small fields.

Turn left at the top of the car park at the entrance to **Presillas Bajas** and, passing above the threshing circle, head along Calle Perdigal. At the end of the street drop down to the left of Finca La Cuesta on a rough concrete track then, maintaining your course where the road arcs left, you reach a signboard for Sendero Caldera Majada

Redonda, SLA101. Continue along the dry bed of the **rambla**, occasionally angling right or left at marker posts to cut corners in its looping course.

Passing beneath the ruined farm of **Cortijo Los Berengueles** (**25min**) and a ruined well, the *rambla* arcs right. When it loops left once more angle up a narrow footpath which soon drops back to the dry river bed. After angling right once more at a marker post the path again returns to the *rambla*, where it reaches the wreck of a car, piled with rocks. Here, angling right, continue parallel to the river bed, heading towards the white sphere of an astronomical observatory atop **Cerro Peñones**, visible on the ridge line up ahead. Paths braid and separate here but all basically end up in the same place.

Descending to the river bed once again, you reach a sign 'Fin de Sendero, Caldera de la Majada Redonda' (**45min**), which explains how the vast crater that surrounds you was formed.

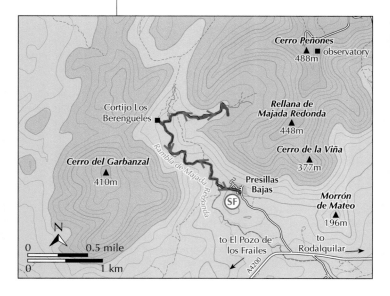

The rambla into the caldera

A **caldera** forms shortly after the eruption of magma from an underground volcano chamber. Large volumes of magma erupt over a short period of time, causing huge damage to the chamber such that it can no longer support its own roof. The roof collapses into the chamber, leaving a huge depression such as you see here. Such chambers can range from 1km to dozens of kilometres in diameter. The depression formed appears to look like a crater in the more traditional sense but is actually a form of sinkhole formed through subsidence, rather than an explosion or impact. Calderas are quite rare.

From the sign continue along the *rambla* for 150m then angle right to reach a low bluff. From here cut right up an indistinct path along the spine of a ridge to reach a higher bluff, marked with a small circle of rocks piled some 50cm high, at the centre of the vast crater of Majada Redonda (**55min**). From the ridge top retrace your steps back to Cortijo Los Berengueles – it's worth making a short diversion to see its ancient threshing floor – and from there back to the beginning of the walk (**1hr 50min**).

WALK 37
Los Escullos circuit via San José

Start/finish	Hotel Los Escullos, Los Escullos
Distance	18km
Ascent/descent	400m
Grade	Medium/Difficult
Time	5hr
Refreshments	El Pozo de los Frailes and San José
Access	From El Pozo de los Frailes take the AL4200 towards Rodalquilar. After approximately 4km turn right at a sign for Chaman/Los Escullos 200m. Continue to the large parking area in front of Hotel Los Escullos.

This longish day-walk circumnavigates the volcanic massif of Los Frailes, whose geological origin is explained on a signboard near the beginning of the walk.

Following the dry bed of the Rambla de la Capitan inland, the route leads you past the ancient water wheel of Cortijos Grandes before reaching the village of El Pozo de los Frailes, named after the Dominican friars who once lived in the area. From here a second *rambla* leads you on to San José where, cutting round the northern edge of the town, you pick up a rocky track which, running high above the Mediterranean, leads you back to Los Escullos.

If you wish to swim, you pass the beach of Cala Higuera just beyond San José or, towards the end of the walk, you could follow a steep path down to the lovely cove of Cala Chica.

The walk begins in front of **Hotel Los Escullos** at the edge of the hamlet of Los Escullos. With your back to the hotel head inland along a broad dirt track, past a sign 'Sendero Escullos-Pozo de los Frailes 5km'. Soon the track angles right and passes a signboard explaining how the the volcanos of Los Frailes were formed.

The path takes you into the *rambla* bed and then to a left fork with a wooden marker post. Angle left for 10m

then, angling right once more, cross the **Rambla de la Capitana** (dry) via a concrete bridge. At the end of the bridge cut left through a big metal gate and continue along a narrow path which, reaching the wall of **Camping Los Escullos**, angles left and widens. Reaching the end of the wall, the track angles left then right and runs alongside the dry river bed, shortly passing to the right of an unfinished building.

Leaving the stream bed you meet a footpath. Here, angling right, continue towards a house grafted onto a vane-less windmill. The path crosses from side to side of the *barranco*. Merging with a broader track bear right for 80m then angle back left and continue parallel to the right bank of the *rambla* on a footpath that soon descends to follow the dry course of the river. Soon you reach the tiny hamlet of **Los Cortijos Grandes**. Here, reaching a row of low, white posts, cut right for 40m to a signboard and one of the park's best preserved **norias de sangre** (literally, 'blood-powered water wheels').

Norias de sangre were so named to differentiate them from wind or water-powered mills. Beasts of burden – mules, donkeys and occasionally oxen – were used to turn the wheels, which brought water to the surface. More than a hundred of the mills have

Restored Norias de Sangre at Pozo de los Frailes

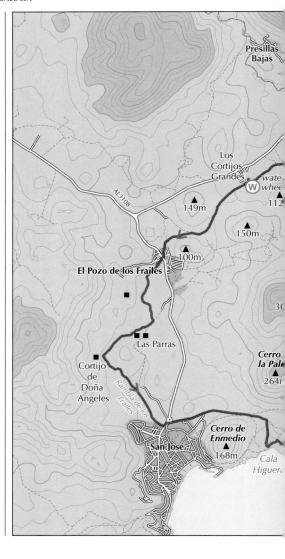

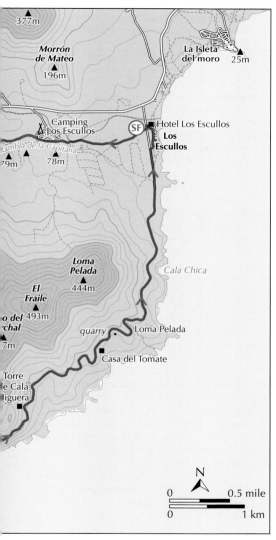

377m

Morrón de Mateo
196m

La Isleta del moro 25m

Camping Los Escullos

SF

Hotel Los Escullos

Los Escullos

Rambla de la Capitana

79m

78m

Loma Pelada
444m

Cala Chica

El Fraile

o del
chal 493m

7m

quarry

Loma Pelada

Casa del Tomate

Torre
e Cala
iguera

N

0   0.5 mile

0   1 km

been catalogued in the Cabo de Gata region. They were first used in Spain during the Moorish period.

Returning to the footpath, you soon leave the last houses of the hamlet behind as you follow a line of agave along the dry bed of the *rambla*. Climbing gently, you cross a low rise then pass two large cairns, where the path widens to become a track, which now runs gently downhill. On reaching a fork, keep left, following way-marking posts with white arrows to enter the village of **El Pozo de los Frailes**.

Entering the village initially along Calle Huerta, follow the main road as it turns right into Calle El Nene and leads down to the main road **AL3108**. Head straight across, passing to the right of a bus stop. ◄ Reaching a sign for Calle Fraile, angle slightly right, cross a children's play area then pick up a broad track which runs parallel to the *rambla* to your left.

Here you will find a perfectly restored *norias de sangre*.

The track gradually arcs round to the left. Keeping left at the next fork, continue along the main track, which soon merges with the *rambla*. Passing beneath power lines, continue along the river bed, passing walls which shore up its banks. Reaching a junction with a broader track, turn right and head on past a large water tank, another water wheel, then the houses (**1hr 35min**) of **Las Parras** (marked on some maps as Cortijo de Pascual).

Following a line of olives, the tracks loops over a low rise then, just before it reaches **Cortijo de Doña Angeles**, angles left and descends. After passing a water treatment plant the track runs on parallel to the **Rambla de los Frailes** to reach the outskirts of **San José** and the **AL3108** (**2hr 15min**). Cut left for 75m then take the first turning to the right. Reaching Bar La Raspa, head along the northern edge of the village, following a broad, quiet road lined with white lamp posts.

Passing the last houses of San José tarmac gives way to dirt. Continue along a broad track that heads east towards the Torre de Cala Higuera, visible high on a hilltop to the east. After a steep climb you reach a three-way junction. Take the middle track, then at the next junction turn right

*San José seen from
Como Pelada*

and head down towards the beach, where you reach a parking area. Heading straight along a narrow path, you cross a broader track to reach **Cala Higuera** (**2hr 50min**).

Leaving the *cala*, retrace your steps for a few metres to the last track you crossed, then cut right in a northeasterly direction to reach a signboard 'Sendero Loma Pelada SLA103'. Here cut right up a path waymarked with white, blue and green posts. On reaching a junction, turn left and follow the path as it angles left across the hillside, shortly reaching the back wall of a villa. Here cut right at a marker post up a steep narrow path which angles right and passes a signboard '**Torre de Cala Higuera**'.

Views open out towards San José as the path, climbing steeply, merges with a broader track which cuts gradually round the hillside. The track, hewn out of solid rock, climbs past a promontory then levels as it adopts a more easterly course, passing beneath a cliff face (Miocene Beach) where two distinct rock strata are very clearly visible. Looping on round the hillside, loose underfoot at this stage, the track passes through a breach in the hillside then passes the ruined building of **Casa del Tomate** then arcs round the edge of a **quarry**.

237

Cala Chica

If you wish to visit Cala Chica be aware that the last section of the path involves using hands as well as feet. It takes about 10 minutes to get down to the beach.

Beyond the quarry the track passes through another breach in the hillside then angles hard left, then back to the right, before reaching **Loma Pelada**, which is worth climbing for great views along the seaboard. From here continue along the track, which shortly begins to descend towards Los Escullos as the headland beyond Las Negras comes into view.

Reaching a signboard 'El Paisaje Sumergido de Cabo de Gata' (describing the rich diversity of the Cabo de Gata marine reserve) (**4hr 25min**), you'll see a path cutting down to the beach of **Cala Chica**. ◄

The track descends and passes a stone obelisk then another signboard about the Reserva Marina Cabo de Gata. The track bears slightly left as it passes Cala Embarcadero, now heading towards the Castillo de Felipe and running just to the left of a wooden fence. Where the fence ends cut right towards the castle then angle left past a neatly dressed stone wall. It is worth walking out and around the seaward side of the fort for the spectacular cliff formations above the foaming sea. Continue past the entrance to the Chaman club then angle left at the Hostal Casa Emilio to return to your point of departure (**5hr**).

WALK 38

Rodalquilar circuit via Cortijo del Fraile

Start/finish	By the gates of the Jardín Botánico just beyond the church in Rodalquilar
Distance	19km; 21km if visiting Cala Los Toros
Ascent/descent	575m
Grade	Medium/Difficult
Time	5hr 20min; 6hr if visiting Cala Los Toros
Refreshments	None en route
Access	Arriving from the AL4200, take any entrance to the village then follow signs to the Punta de Información, which is next to the church. There's parking just beyond the church, in front of the gates to the Vivero Rodalquilar.

This fascinating, circular walk takes in the haunting beauty of the Cabo de Gata hinterland, as well as the stark hillsides above the abandoned Rodalquilar gold mines, before returning to the village via two remote *ramblas* and the volcanic plain to the south of Rodalquilar.

An added, slightly surreal bonus is a side trip to the abandoned farm of Cortijo del Fraile: the dramatic events that took place here in the 1930s inspired one of Federico García Lorca's most famous works. This is a walk of enormous contrasts, which could easily be stretched out over a whole day, especially if you choose to visit the beautiful beach of Cala Los Toros.

With your back to the gates of the Vivero Rodalquilar, which is just beyond the church in Rodalquilar, turn left and head up the hill. The road angles right then left and passes a number of disused mine buildings. On reaching a sign 'Ruta de la Minería' cut left just before a café, following a metal railing. The road arcs right then, reverting to dirt, passes around and behind the Rodalquilar **mine factory**, where a signboard explains how gold was extracted from the mined ore.

Gold was discovered by accident in lead smelt-ings at Rodalquilar at the end of the 19th century.

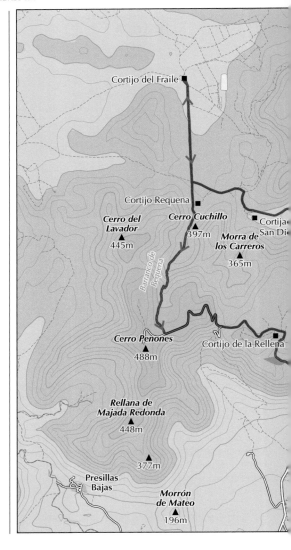

The disused goldmines of Rodalquilar

Attempts by two different companies to refine the metal using the mercury process were doomed to failure, but a third attempt, this time using the cyanidation method, proved successful. The mines, which were nationalised after the Civil War, were eventually closed in 1966.

The track climbs gradually, marked with marker posts with white arrows. After passing a ruined building the track cuts beneath overhead power cables. Climbing higher, you pass to the right of the abandoned buildings of **Cortijada San Diego**, where you'll see a mine shaft to your right, and shortly afterwards, another to the left.

On reaching a junction, bear left, sticking to the most clearly defined track, signed with white-arrowed waymarking posts. Passing through a breach in the hillside, the track descends before levelling and reaching a crossroads where the tracks to your left and right are lined with agave (**55min**). Turn right following a sign 'Sendero Cortijo del Fraile'. After 1.4km you reach the buildings of **Cortijo del Fraile**. After visiting the farm retrace your steps back to the crossroads you reached at 55min (**1hr 45min**).

The events that took place in 1928 at **Cortijo del Fraile**, which was built by Dominican friars in the 18th century, were the inspiration for Federico Lorca's *Bodas de Sangre*.

The young daughter of the farm's owner, Francisca, was due to be married to a farm labourer who she despised. She eloped just hours before the wedding with her cousin but the groom-to-be's brother shot him dead and severely injured Francisca as they fled the farm. She lived the remainder of her life as a recluse, unaware of the existence of Lorca's play.

The buildings have served as a location for some well-known films: notably, as the mission in *The Good, the Bad and the Ugly* (1966) and as a hideout in *For a Few Dollars More* (1965). Other Westerns with scenes there include *A Bullet for the General* (1966), *Last of the Badmen* (1967), *Ace High* (1968), *A Long Ride from Hell* (1968), *Blood and Guns* (1969) and *Silver Saddle* (1978).

On reaching the junction, head straight across past a signboard for Sendero Requena. Following a line of

Cortijo del Fraile

agave for 600m, you reach the farm of **Cortijo Requena**. Passing to the right of the farm, you pick up a track that runs up the right bank of the **Barranco de Requena**: soon you'll see the white globe of an astronomical observatory on the ridge up ahead. Running up the right bank of the stream, the track, passing between two fenced enclosures, narrows to become a path, which soon crosses to the stream's left bank. Climbing more steeply across rocks it then crosses back over the stream. Angling back to the stream's left bank once more you pass a signboard about the Barranco de Requena and its flora (**2hr 35min**).

After 40m the path crosses to the stream's right bank before angling left once more and crossing to the far bank. Reaching an area more denuded of vegetation, the path angles left. Crossing a dry stream bed, you reach a track where views open out towards the sea. Here turn left.

The track passes to the left of a phone mast, angles right, then passes left of a second mast. Looping steeply downhill, the track passes through a stone-posted gate. Here jink left to go straight on (the main track cuts sharply right), following waymarking. ◄

The track now runs across a more open area whose old terraces bear testimony to the fact that the land was once under cultivation.

After passing between two 60s-style gateposts the track passes just to the left of the **Cortijo de la Rellena** then runs briefly towards three spectral houses on the skyline. After running towards the middle house the track loops hard right. After 80m cut right at a marker post and informational signboard and leave the track along a narrow path which descends through a stand of pine trees. Reaching the (dry) stream bed, follow on down the path, which loops to and fro across the river before passing a signboard for Sendero Requena. Here, cutting left, you reach the **AL4200** (**4hr 10min**), where you should turn left. After 50m you reach a parking area to the right of the road.

If you wish to visit **Cala Los Toros**, cut right at a cairn and follow a track down towards the sea. On reaching a sign for Cala Los Toros, angle left along a narrow path then follow the dry river bed down to the beach. Retrace your steps back up to the AL4200. Allow 40min extra for this diversion.

Continue east along the AL4200. The road loops left as it passes **Mirador de la Amatista** – it's worth a short diversion – then, crossing a rise, begins to descend. Where the road levels look to the left for a green-and-white sign for Punta de Información, La Amatista. Opposite the sign cut right and leave the AL4200 via a narrow footpath marked with blue and white waymarking.

Reaching a junction with a broader track, head straight across, looking for blue and white paint splashes on rocks at the roadside. At the next junction cut left along a track that runs straight towards Rodalquilar. Passing to the left of a newly built house, the track runs up to meet the AL4200. Head straight across, along a less distinct track.

Continue past some quirky smallholdings into the village. Descending and crossing a (dry) stream bed, you reach a junction in front of house number 30. Here turn left along Calle Santa Bárbara and continue past a line of restaurants to reach another junction. Here turn right. After some 200m you arrive back at the walk's start point (**5hr 20min**).

The path up the Barranco de Requena

WALK 39
Las Negras circuit via El Playazo

Start/finish	The roundabout with palm trees at the northern entrance to Las Negras
Distance	16km
Ascent/descent	350m
Grade	Medium
Time	4hr 30min
Refreshments	Las Negras
Access	Las Negras is well signed from the main A7 motorway at Níjar. Follow the AL3106 before turning left (signed) just before the village. Park on the outskirts. It is a small place so only a short stroll to the start.

Las Negras is the least developed of the coastal settlements of Cabo de Gata. It remains a quiet backwater in all but the summer months, with a friendly and laid-back vibe in its beachside bars and restaurants.

This walk first explores the haunting beauty of the *ramblas* that run past the northern and eastern flanks of the Cerro de las Hortichuelas before descending to El Playazo's enchanting sweep of beach lined with swaying palm trees and deserted for most of the year. The final part of the walk, by way of the path known to locals as El Sendero de la Molata, is one of the most beautiful sections of the coastal path that runs all the way along Cabo de Gata's seaboard. Set time aside for a leisurely picnic on the beach and to visit the restored water wheel you pass just before reaching the sea.

From the roundabout head down Calle Bahía de las Negras. On reaching the beach, turn right along the sand, passing beneath Restaurante La Barcas then Bar Manteca. Cross a dry river bed then cut right at the end of a wooden fence to reach a tarmac road. Here angle left and follow the track over the brow of a hill into the bay of **Cala del Cuervo**.

Reaching the second set of bollards, angle left to cut a corner then rejoin the road. After 25m cut left again and drop down, parallel to a fence. Reaching a sign for

Cala del Cuervo, angle right and follow a track along the dry **Rambla de Cala de Cuervo**, passing to the right of **We Camp**.

At times it is much easier to walk alongside the *rambla* rather than in it. Passing white then pink-coloured buildings, the track angles right before running up to the **AL3106** (**50min**). Crossing the road, maintain your course along the lower of two tracks that runs on along the *rambla*, passing beneath a line of houses. Reaching an open, concreted area, angle left uphill, to reach a larger, open tarmac area that might pass as the village centre of **Las Hortichuelas**. Keep trending left to walk down Calle Mayor.

At the end of the street bear right past the last of the hamlet's houses to reach a stop sign and the AL3106. Turn right along the road then after 175m angle left at a sign 'Atención, Carretera Cortada'. The road climbs then angles right along the eastern flank of the **Cerro de las Hortichuelas**, soon passing to the left of a white building, where the track becomes more rutted. ▸

Waymarking posts with red triangles and dots plot your course.

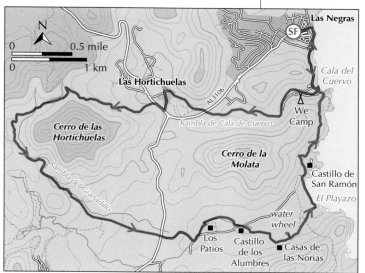

247

Track beneath Cerro de las Hortichuelas

Levelling out, the track reaches a wooden post with signs pointing left and right for the E01 footpath. Here angle back hard left down a less distinct track that soon leads you across two dry *ramblas*. Becoming rockier the track angles left, running back towards the sea. After crossing an *era* (threshing area) it arcs right then descends into the **Rambla del Granadillo**, where it runs past an old water tank.

Adopting a course higher above the Granadillo's right bank, you pass above a second tank. The track narrows to become a footpath, which runs past a group of ruined corrals, still hugging the Granadilla's right bank. After descending back to the *rambla* continue along the dry bed for 60m then angle right and continue on above its right bank. ◄

The valley widens as the Torre de los Lobos watchtower comes into sight to the southeast.

Reaching a fork in the track, keep left. The track angles away from the *rambla* as it runs on across a flat plain, passing to the right of a ruin. Reaching the AL4200, angle slightly right, cross the road and head down a concreted track, following signs for El Playazo and Los Patios.

The track bears left, right then left again as it passes an old (vane-less) windmill.

On reaching the point where the track crosses the *rambla*, just before a 20km sign, cut left along the *rambla*'s right bank. Reaching the buildings of **Los Patios**, angle left then right into the bed of the *rambla*, now heading towards the tower of the Castillo de los Alumbres (marked Castillo de Rodalquilar on some maps).

Reaching the concrete track you left earlier, head straight across, following the *rambla*'s gravelly bed, passing around to the left of the **Castillo de los Alumbres**, to reach another broad track. ▶ Here, angling left towards the sea, you soon pass to the right of a plantation of palm trees. The track passes an old water wheel then angles right, towards the buildings of **Casas de las Norias**. Here the track bears left and, passing some 75m right of a recently restored **water wheel**, reaches the palm-fringed beach of El Playazo (**2hr 55min**).

Heading straight across a track and passing between two metal signs, one for Playa El Playazo, the other No

An alternative to the *rambla*'s gravel is simply to carry on taking the concrete track all the way to the car park at the beach's eastern end. It's easier underfoot but does miss out on both the water wheel and much of the bay.

The restored water wheel of Casas de las Norias

entry, you reach the beach. Reaching the harder sand at the ocean's edge, turn left and head to the far end of the bay, where you'll see two white buildings. Pass between the two buildings then angle right then left up a narrow, rocky path. On reaching a track, bear right towards the Castillo de San Ramón to reach a signboard for Sendero La Molata. Here cut left up a waymarked path. After crossing a gully via a wooden bridge the path passes behind the **Castillo de San Ramón**.

> The **Castillo de San Ramón** was part of an elaborate line of coastal defences that was built at the end of the 18th century during the reign of Charles III. A battery of four cannons at the front of the castle controlled access to the bay of El Playazo. After being damaged by the French during the War of Independence it was eventually sold by the state in 1875 for 1500 pesetas. The castle is now a private home.

On reaching a fork keep right and climb steeply past a signboard that details the geology of Cerro de la Molata. Passing a breach in the hillside, the path loops down towards **Cala del Cuervo**, from where you retrace your steps back to Las Negras and a well-deserved drink at La Bodeguiya right on the foreshore (**4hr 30min**).

The bay of El Playazo

WALK 40

Agua Amarga to Las Negras

Start	The roundabout at the entrance of Agua Amarga, next to a sign for Sendero 450m
Finish	Las Negras
Distance	13.5km; 20km Agua Amarga to San Pedro and back
Ascent/descent	550m; 800m Agua Amarga to San Pedro and back
Grade	Medium; Medium/Difficult Agua Amarga to San Pedro and back
Time	4hr 15min; 6hr Agua Amarga to San Pedro and back
Refreshments	None en route
Access	Agua Amarga is accessed via the AL5106 that runs east–west across the top of the town. Parking is ample just outside the main village.

The cliff path linking the seaside village of Agua Amarga with the smaller coastal settlement of Las Negras, via three of the park's most beautiful coves, is a highlight of any visit to Cabo de Gata. Unlike most walks described in this guide, this is a linear route: circuits based on this itinerary are very poor cousins. But a taxi back to the walk's start point from Las Negras (there's no public transport) costs just €40.

You could also make this a there-and-back hike to the beach of San Pedro, one of southern Europe's top candidates for the title of The Beach. This remote cove is inhabited for part of the year by a friendly bunch of hippies who happily smoke their weed among the rocks. Set out early, take a picnic and set time aside for a leisurely swim and picnic beneath San Pedro's 16th-century watchtower, which once protected this part of the coast from raids by Barbary pirates.

The walk begins in Agua Amarga next to the sign for Sendero 450m, at the northern entrance to the village. From the sign follow a tarmac road uphill which bears right then climbs steeply, marked with blue and white waymarking flashes, up to another sign for Sendero 200m by a brick hut, both covered in graffiti. Ignore the Fin de

251

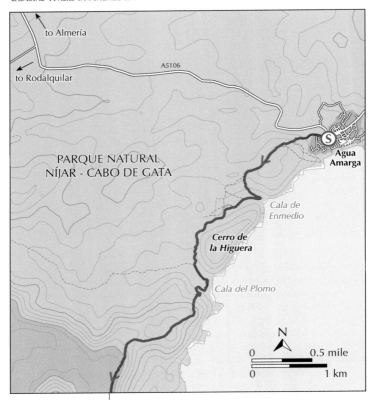

map continues
on page 254

Sendero sign. Here head straight ahead, up a rough dirt track which passes two transmitter masts before reaching a flatter area, where a signboard marks the beginning of the walk. Head straight up a ridge on a path that climbs steeply as great views open out across the bay of Agua Amarga and north to the Cabo de Gata hinterland.

Reaching a fork, keep left, following a painted arrow on a rock, and pass through a breach in the ridge (**30min**), beyond which the path drops down to the beach of **Cala de Enmedio** (**40min**).

After visiting the beach head inland along a track. Where it divides keep left, along a better-defined track, heading inland, just to the left of a *rambla*. As you approach an ugly farm building where the track angles right, cut left along a footpath, which at first hugs the left side of the *barranco* before it climbs away from its dry course, passes behind **Cerro de la Higuera**, then descends into the valley leading to the Cala del Plomo, where it meets with a track. A finger sign for Cala Enmedio 1.5km points back the way you've come. Turning left, you soon reach the beach and the small cluster of houses of **Cala del Plomo** (**1hr 20min**).

Reaching the beach, the track angles right and passes a green barrier blocking access to cars. After 30m, as the track cuts right, continue straight on at a scruffy painted sign for Sendero Cala San Pedro. From here the path narrows and loops right, above the highest houses of the hamlet, then climbs steeply upwards before it angles back towards the sea. After passing beneath a rocky

The coast path between Cala del Plomo and Cala de San Pedro

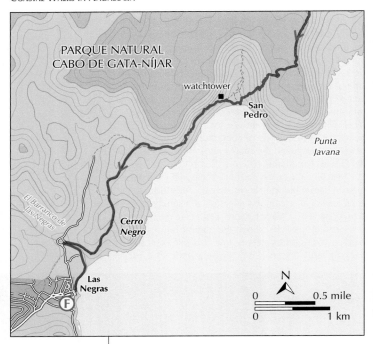

outcrop the path levels as it runs between tall grasses across a flat area. After climbing once again it levels, now running close to a steep cliff face, which is to your left.

After running close to the cliff face the path, now marked with occasional blue and white markings, angles sharply right and away from the sea. Angling left once more, back towards the sea, you cross a rise, at which point the eye-wateringly beautiful Cala de San Pedro comes into sight. From here the path descends in a series of steep loops towards the old watchtower at its eastern end. Reaching the valley floor, cut left at a lower watchtower, then, passing a rectilinear, flat-roofed house, drop down to the **San Pedro** beach via a flight of steps (**2hr 55min**).

The footpath leading down to Cala de San Pedro

The watchtower at Cala de San Pedro

After rest and recuperation on the beach you could retrace your footsteps back to Agua Amarga (**6hr**).

If you intend to head all the way to Las Negras, angle right along the beach passing the mouth of its (dry) river, looking for a gap in the coastal scrub. From here steps lead up to the beach's ancient **watchtower**. After reaching the eastern side of the tower, and angling right, you reach San Pedro's spring and a signboard exhorting visitors to treat the beach as if it were their own, plus a swing.

The **watchtower of San Pedro**, originally built to protect the coastline from raids by North African pirates, was damaged in 1743 by an English man-of-war, which had given chase to a Spanish pirate ship from Málaga. After attacking the Spanish ship and disabling several fishing boats that were anchored in the bay, the English ship fired on the tower. It was never repaired.

From the spring head west to pick up the continuation of the footpath, which angles gradually up across the mountainside. At a point where the path widens you reach a fork where, angling slightly right, you can continue along a narrower path which runs parallel to the one you were following, which is now just to your left. On reaching another fork, cut left to reach a broader track and a marker post. Here, continuing on the same course, you pass through a breach in the mountains as you head on towards Las Negras.

Passing behind the black volcanic massif of **Cerro Negro**, the track angles right and descends to the houses at the northeastern edge of **Las Negras**. Passing a signboard for Cala de San Pedro, then a chain blocking vehicular access, after 50m cut left and follow the dry river bed of **El Barranco de las Negras** down to the pebbly beach. Follow the track as it angles right past an old pillbox and runs parallel to the sea past the first houses of the village. The walk ends in front of house number 34, next to La Bodeguiya, a lively bar that gives out great tapas free with drinks: it's an excellent spot to celebrate the end of a fine walk (**4hr 15min**).

TAXIS

Taxis pick up at the bus stop, reached by turning inland at La Bodeguiya to a roundabout with a circle of palm trees. The bus stop is to the right of the roundabout. The fare in 2024 was €40. Taxi: tel 671 24 40 65 or 636 79 11 27 (Ricardo).

APPENDIX A
Useful contacts

Many of the following websites are in Spanish by default, but most include the option of an English-language version at the click of a button.

Transport

Train
Renfe (national rail operator)
tel (+34) 912 32 03 20
www.renfe.com

Tourist information

Costa de la Luz
Vejer de la Frontera Tourist Office
Avenida. Los Remedios, 2
11150
www.turismovejer.es

Tarifa Tourist Office
Paseo de la Alameda, s/n
https://tarifaturismo.com/
oficina-de-turismo-tarifa/

Costa del Sol and Gibraltar
Gibraltar Tourist Office
13 John Mackintosh Square
www.visitgibraltar.gi

Estepona Tourist Office
Plaza de las Flores, s/n
29680
https://turismo.estepona.es

Marbella Tourist Office
Plaza de Los Naranjos
29601
www.andalucia.com

Mijas Tourist Office
Plaza Virgen de la Peña, 2A
29650
https://turismo.mijas.es

Costa Tropical
Frigiliana Tourist Office
Calle Cuesta del Apero, 10
29788
www.turismofrigiliana.es

Costa de Almería
San José Tourist Office
Avenida de San José, 27
www.cabogataalmeria.com

Maps

In Andalucía
LTC
Avenida Menéndez Pelayo, 42–44
41003 Sevilla

Mapas y Compañia
Calle Compañía, 33
29008 Málaga
www.mapasycia.es

In Madrid
Centro Nacional de Información Geográfica
Calle del General Ibáñez de Ibero, 3
28003 Madrid
www.cnig.es

In the UK
Stanfords
7 Mercer Walk
Covent Garden
London WC2H 9FA
www.stanfords.co.uk

Birdwatching and wildlife
The Andalucía Bird Society is a great first stop for anybody interested in the birdlife of the area.
www.andaluciabirdsociety.org

The terrace of the Hotel Los Altos de Istán

Spanish Nature provides organised birding tours and walks in Andalucía and further afield. Contact Peter Jones via the website:
www.spanishnature.com

The Iberia Nature Forum provides comprehensive information, news and discussion about the plants and wildlife of the region.
www.iberianatureforum.com

Emergency services
Emergency services (general)
tel 112

Guardia Civil (police)
tel 062

Local police
tel 092

Medical emergencies
tel 061

Fire service
tel 080

British Consulate General (Madrid)
tel (+34) 917 14 63 00

APPENDIX B
Accommodation

○ Hotel   ♦ Hostel/   ○ B&B/   ○ Self catering
              Bunkhouse   Guesthouse

Location	Name	Type	Web
Parque Natural de la Breña y las Marismas			
Vejer de la Frontera	La Casa del Califa €€–€€€	○	www.califavejer.com
	Hotel Convento San Francisco €€	○	www.tugasa.com
Los Caños de Meca	Hotel Madreselva €€	○	www.califavejer.com
	Hotel La Breña €€	○	www.hotelbrena.com
Parques Naturales de Los Alcornocales y del Estrecho			
Bolonia	Hostal La Hormiga Voladora €–€€	♦ ○	www.lahormigavoladora.com
	Hostal Ríos €–€€	○ ○	www.hostalriosbolonia.com
El Pelayo	Huerta Grande €–€€	○	www.huertagrande.com
Tarifa	Hostal Alameda €€	♦	www.hostalalameda.com
Paraje Natural de Sierra Bermeja y Sierra Crestellina			
Casares	Hotel Rural Casares €–€€	○	www.hotelcasares.es
	Las Casitas de mi Abuela €€	○	https://lascasitasdemiabuela.com
Sabinillas	Hotel Don Agustín €	○	www.hoteldonagustin.com
La Sierra Blanca, Parque Nacional de La Sierra de Las Nieves			
In the park	Refugio de Juanar €€–€€€	○	www.elrefugiodejuanar.com

The following price ranges are intended as a guideline only. You may find lower prices out of season or by shopping around on the internet.

€   less than €60 for a double room
€€   between €60 and €110 for a double room
€€€   more than €110 for a double room

omments

eautiful bedrooms with a restaurant offering a mix of Mediterranean and Eastern cuisine

xcellent choice at the heart of the old town, with mid-week deals

ruce small hotel with pool and courtyard-facing rooms

iendly hotel close to the start of the Caños cliff path, with excellent restaurant

mple and enchanting hostel at the ocean's edge

nother cheap-and-cheerful *pensión* with a number of ocean-facing rooms

g cabins hidden in among cork oaks, a great base for any of the local walks

ean and friendly hostel with restaurant at the edge of the old town

expensive hotel at the heart of the village, with quiet rooms

vo charming self-catered accommodation units in the heart of the old town. Good value.

iendly small hotel next to the beach and close to all walks

perfect base for your sorties with traditional Andalusian cuisine

Location	Name	Type	Web
Istán	Hotel Los Jarales €–€€	⌂	www.losjarales.com
	Hotel Altos de Istán €€–€€€	⌂	www.hotelaltosdeistan.com
Ojén	La Posada del Angel €€	⌂	www.laposadadelangel.es
La Sierra de Mijas			
Benalmádena Pueblo	La Posada €–€€	⌂	www.iambenalmadena.com
	La Fonda €€–€€€	⌂	www.lafondabenalmadena.es
Mijas Pueblo	El Escudo de Mijas €–€€	⌂	www.el-escudo.com
Parque Natural Sierras de Tejeda, Almijara y Alhama			
Cómpeta	Hotel Balcón de Cómpeta €€	⌂	www.hotel-competa.com
Canillas de Albaida	Posada La Plaza €–€€	⌂	www.posada-laplaza.com
	Finca El Cerrillo €€–€€€	⌂	www.hotelfinca.com
Maro	Hotel Restaurante Playa Maro €–€€	⌂ ⌂	www.hotelplayamaro.com
Frigiliana	Millers of Frigiliana €€–€€€	⌂	www.millershotels.com
Parque Natural de Níjar-Cabo de Gata			
Rodalquilar	El Jardín de los Sueños €€	⌂	www.eljardindelossuenos.es
	Los Patios €€€	⌂	www.lospatioshotel.es
Agua Amarga	Hostal Family €€	⌂	www.familyaguaamarga.com
Las Negras	Hotel Cala Chica €€€	⌂	https://hotelesarrecife.es/calachica
San José	Doña Pakyta €€€	⌂	www.playasycortijos.com

omments

expensive and friendly family-run hotel just south of Istán

ewly refurbished and reopened smart hotel above the village, with outstanding views

harming small hotel with 17 pretty bedrooms decorated in an angelic theme

bulous small hotel in a quiet back street. Excellent value for money.

reat location at the edge of the village with views down to the Mediterranean

um in the village centre, pretty rooms and good deals in low season

iendly mid-range hotel with a pool and views out towards the sea

omfortable and welcoming hotel in the pretty square of Canillas de Albaida

bulous small rural hotel with great food and very friendly British hosts. Dinner is available at
e hotel five evenings a week.

mple 3-star hostelry on the eastern side of the village, with pool

eautifully renovated boutique hotel in the heart of the old moorish quarter. Individually
signed suites and rooms.

ural B&B with excellent breakfasts and a volcano-facing pool and gardens

perb small hotel with gourmet cuisine, next to the track leading to the Playazo beach

ench-run restaurant with rooms, just back from the Agua Amarga beach

cellent hotel about 150m back from the beach of Las Negras

cellent hotel with sea views, close to the start point of the San José circuit: worth a splurge

APPENDIX C
Glossary

Spanish	English
acequia	man-made irrigation channel: many of those in Andalucía date from the Moorish period
alcornoques	cork oaks
almiñar	minaret
almadraba	the annual tuna catch on Andalucía's Atlantic Coast
arroyo	stream
ayuntamiento	town hall
barranco	gorge or canyon of the type found in the Alpujarras
cala	small bay with a beach
calera	pit where lime was made by firing limestone
cañada	drovers' road and public right of way
canuto	steep-sided gorge where a warm, humid climate fosters extraordinarily diverse flora
capilla	chapel
casa forestal	forestry department building
cerro	peak or mountain
choza	simple hut or dwelling, often with thatched roof
cortijo	farm
consultorio	doctor's surgery
coto (de caza)	hunting reserve
dehesa	forest which has been partially cleared to leave selected species eg evergreen and cork
era	threshing area, often circular
guiri	foreigner (slang)
GR	abbreviation for Gran Recorrido or Long-Distance Footpath
huerta	small patch of cultivated land
humilladero	small mountain shrine
ingenio	factory where sugar was manufactured from sugar cane
laja	jagged ridge formed when limestone strata run vertically upwards
marisma	marsh
mirador	viewing point
puerto	mountain pass
rambla	dry river bed
secadero	flat platforms used in La Axarquía for laying out grapes in the sunshine

APPENDIX D
Further reading

Plants and wildlife
A good field guide to the birds and flowers of the area will enrich any walk in Andalucía. The better-known field guides, which are nearly all easily available in the UK and via the internet, include the following:

Botanical guides
Marjorie Blamey and Christopher Grey-Wilson, *Wild Flowers of the Mediterranean*, A&C Black, 2004.

Paul Davies and Bob Gibbons, *Field Guide to Wild Flowers of Southern Europe*, The Crowood Press Ltd, 1993. A comprehensive work of manageable size.

Betty Molesworth Allen, A Selection of *Wildflowers of Southern Spain*, Santana Books, 2005. A great local field guide, although difficult to find. Lists Spanish names as well as medicinal/culinary uses of plants described and local folklore related to different species.

Oleg Polunin and BE Smythies, *Flowers of South-west Europe: A Field Guide*, Oxford University Press, 1988. Very comprehensive: this is a classic botanical must-have.

Ornithological guides
Peterson, Mountfort and Hollom, *A Field Guide to the Birds of Britain and Europe*, Houghton Mifflin Harcourt, 2001.

Lars Svensson, Killian Mullarney and Dan Zetterstom, *Birds of Europe*, Princeton University Press, 2010.

Lars Svensson, Killian Mullarney and Dan Zetterstom, *Collins Bird Guide*, Collins, 2010.

Andalucía fact and fiction

Gibraltar
René Chartrand, *Gibraltar 1779–83 The Great Siege*, Osprey Publishing, 2006. The story of the four-year-long siege by land and sea of the Rock by the French and Spanish.

Costa Tropical
David Baird, *East of Málaga*, Santana Books, 2008. A great general guide to just about every aspect of La Axarquía.

David Baird, *Between Two Fires*, Maroma Press, 2011. How a guerrilla resistance group fought the Franco regime in the mountains just back from the coastline of La Axarquía following the Civil War.

Spain general
Gerald Brenan, *The Spanish Labyrinth*, Cambridge University Press, 2015. One of the best overviews of the conflict that ripped Spain apart in the late 1930s.

Antony Beevor, *The Battle for Spain: The Spanish Civil War 1936–39*, W&N, 2006.

Richard Fletcher, *Moorish Spain*, University of California Press, 2006. An insightful account of an age that transformed Spanish culture and society.

John Gill, *Andalucía, A Cultural History*, Signal Books, 2008. A quirky and highly personal take on all things Andaluz.

DOWNLOAD THE GPX FILES

All the routes in this guide are available for download from:

www.cicerone.co.uk/1265/GPX

as standard format GPX files. You should be able to load them into most online GPX systems and mobile devices, whether GPS or smartphone. You may need to convert the file into your preferred format using a conversion programme such as gpsvisualizer.com or one of the many other such websites and programmes.

When you follow this link, you will be asked for your email address and where you purchased the guidebook, and have the option to subscribe to the Cicerone e-newsletter.

www.cicerone.co.uk

NOTES

LISTING OF CICERONE GUIDES

BRITISH ISLES CHALLENGES, COLLECTIONS AND ACTIVITIES

Great Walks on the England Coast Path
Map and Compass
The Big Rounds
The Book of the Bivvy
The Book of the Bothy
The Mountains of England and Wales:
   Vol 1 Wales
   Vol 2 England
The National Trails
Walking the End to End Trail

SHORT WALKS SERIES

Short Walks Hadrian's Wall
Short Walks Lake District — Keswick, Borrowdale and Buttermere
Short Walks Lake District — Windermere Ambleside and Grasmere
Short Walks Lake District — Coniston and Langdale
Short Walks in Arnside and Silverdale
Short Walks in Nidderdale
Short Walks in Northumberland: Wooler, Rothbury, Alnwick and the coast
Short Walks on the Malvern Hills
Short Walks in Cornwall: Falmouth and the Lizard
Short Walks in Cornwall: Land's End and Penzance
Short Walks in the South Downs: Brighton, Eastbourne and Arundel
Short Walks in the Surrey Hills
Short Walks on Dartmoor — South: Ivybridge and Princetown
Short Walks on Exmoor
Short Walks Winchester
Short Walks in Pembrokeshire: Tenby and the south
Short Walks in Dumfries and Galloway
Short Walks on the Isle of Mull
Short Walks on the Orkney Islands
Short Walks on the Shetland Islands

SCOTLAND

Ben Nevis and Glen Coe
Cycling in the Hebrides
Cycling the North Coast 500
Great Mountain Days in Scotland
Mountain Biking in Southern and Central Scotland
Mountain Biking in West and North West Scotland
Not the West Highland Way Scotland
Scotland's Best Small Mountains

Scotland's Mountain Ridges
Scottish Wild Country Backpacking
Skye's Cuillin Ridge Traverse
The Borders Abbeys Way
The Great Glen Way
The Great Glen Way Map Booklet
The Hebridean Way
The Hebrides
The Isle of Mull
The Isle of Skye
The Skye Trail
The Southern Upland Way
The West Highland Way
Walking Ben Lawers, Rannoch and Atholl
Walking in the Cairngorms
Walking in the Pentland Hills
Walking in the Scottish Borders
Walking in the Southern Uplands
Walking in Torridon, Fisherfield, Fannichs and An Teallach
Walking Loch Lomond and the Trossachs
Walking on Arran
Walking on Harris and Lewis
Walking on Jura, Islay and Colonsay
Walking on Rum and the Small Isles
Walking on the Orkney and Shetland Isles
Walking on Uist and Barra
Walking the Cape Wrath Trail
Walking the Corbetts Vol 1 South of the Great Glen
Walking the Corbetts Vol 2 North of the Great Glen
Walking the Fife Pilgrim Way
Walking the Galloway Hills
Walking the John o' Groats Trail
Walking the Munros
   Vol 1 — Southern, Central and Western Highlands
   Vol 2 — Northern Highlands and the Cairngorms
Walking the West Highland Way
West Highland Way Map Booklet
Winter Climbs in the Cairngorms
Winter Climbs: Ben Nevis and Glen Coe

NORTHERN ENGLAND ROUTES

Cycling the Reivers Route
Cycling the Way of the Roses
Hadrian's Cycleway
Hadrian's Wall Path
Hadrian's Wall Path Map Booklet
The Coast to Coast Cycle Route
The Coast to Coast Map Booklet
The Coast to Coast Walk
The Pennine Way
Pennine Way Map Booklet
Walking the Dales Way
The Dales Way Map Booklet

LAKE DISTRICT

Bikepacking in the Lake District
Cycling in the Lake District
Great Mountain Days in the Lake District
Joss Naylor's Lakes, Meres and Waters of the Lake District
Lake District Winter Climbs
Lake District: High Level and Fell Walks
Lake District: Low Level and Lake Walks
Mountain Biking in the Lake District
Outdoor Adventures with Children — Lake District
Scrambles in the Lake District — North
   South
Trail and Fell Running in the Lake District
Walking The Cumbria Way
Walking the Lake District Fells — Borrowdale
   Buttermere
   Coniston
   Keswick
   Langdale
   Mardale and the Far East
   Patterdale
   Wasdale
Walking the Tour of the Lake District

NORTH-WEST ENGLAND AND THE ISLE OF MAN

Cycling the Pennine Bridleway
Isle of Man Coastal Path
The Lancashire Cycleway
The Lune Valley and Howgills
Walking in Cumbria's Eden Valley
Walking in Lancashire
Walking in the Forest of Bowland and Pendle
Walking on the Isle of Man
Walking on the West Pennine Moors
Walking the Ribble Way
Walks in Silverdale and Arnside

NORTH-EAST ENGLAND, YORKSHIRE DALES AND PENNINES

Cycling in the Yorkshire Dales
Great Mountain Days in the Pennines
Mountain Biking in the Yorkshire Dales
The Cleveland Way and the Yorkshire Wolds Way
The Cleveland Way Map Booklet
The North York Moors
Trail and Fell Running in the Yorkshire Dales
Walking in County Durham

The Camino Portugues
Walking in Portugal
Walking in the Algarve
Walking on Madeira
Walking on the Azores

SWITZERLAND

Switzerland's Jura Crest Trail
The Swiss Alps
Tour of the Jungfrau Region
Trekking the Swiss Via Alpina
Walking in Arolla and Zinal
Walking in the Bernese Oberland — Jungfrau region
Walking in the Engadine — Switzerland
Walking in the Valais
Walking in Ticino
Walking in Zermatt and Saas-Fee

GERMANY

Hiking and Cycling in the Black Forest
The Danube Cycleway Vol 1
The Rhine Cycle Route
The Westweg
Walking in the Bavarian Alps

POLAND, SLOVAKIA, ROMANIA, HUNGARY AND BULGARIA

The Danube Cycleway Vol 2
The High Tatras
The Mountains of Romania

SCANDINAVIA, ICELAND AND GREENLAND

Hiking in Norway — North
Hiking in Norway — South
Trekking the Kungsleden
Trekking in Greenland — The Arctic Circle Trail
Walking and Trekking in Iceland

SLOVENIA, CROATIA, SERBIA, MONTENEGRO AND ALBANIA

Hiking Slovenia's Juliana Trail
Mountain Biking in Slovenia
The Islands of Croatia
The Julian Alps of Slovenia
The Mountains of Montenegro
The Peaks of the Balkans Trail
The Slovene Mountain Trail
Walking in Slovenia: The Karavanke
Walks and Treks in Croatia

ITALY

Alta Via 1 — Trekking in the Dolomites
Alta Via 2 — Trekking in the Dolomites
Day Walks in the Dolomites
Italy's Grande Traversata delle Alpi
Italy's Sibillini National Park
Ski Touring and Snowshoeing in the Dolomites

The Way of St Francis
Trekking Gran Paradiso: Alta Via 2
Trekking in the Apennines
Trekking the Giants' Trail: Alta Via 1 through the Italian Pennine Alps
Via Ferratas of the Italian Dolomites: Vol 1
Vol 2
Walking in Abruzzo
Walking in Italy's Cinque Terre
Walking in Italy's Stelvio National Park
Walking in Sicily
Walking in the Aosta Valley
Walking in the Dolomites
Walking in Tuscany
Walking in Umbria
Walking Lake Como and Maggiore
Walking Lake Garda and Iseo
Walking on the Amalfi Coast
Walking the Via Francigena Pilgrim Route — Part 2
Walking the Via Francigena Pilgrim Route — Part 3
Walks and Treks in the Maritime Alps

IRELAND

The Wild Atlantic Way and Western Ireland
Walking the Kerry Way
Walking the Wicklow Way

EUROPEAN CYCLING

Cycling the Route des Grandes Alpes
Cycling the Ruta Via de la Plata
The Elbe Cycle Route
The River Loire Cycle Route
The River Rhone Cycle Route

INTERNATIONAL CHALLENGES, COLLECTIONS AND ACTIVITIES

Europe's High Points
Walking the Via Francigena Pilgrim Route — Part 1

AUSTRIA

Innsbruck Mountain Adventures
Trekking Austria's Adlerweg
Trekking in Austria's Hohe Tauern
Trekking in Austria's Stubai Alps
Trekking in Austria's Zillertal Alps
Walking in Austria
Walking in the Salzkammergut: the Austrian Lake District

MEDITERRANEAN

The High Mountains of Crete
Trekking in Greece
Walking and Trekking in Zagori
Walking and Trekking on Corfu
Walking on the Greek Islands — the Cyclades
Walking in Cyprus
Walking in Malta

HIMALAYA

8000 metres
Everest: A Trekker's Guide
Trekking in the Karakoram

NORTH AMERICA

Hiking and Cycling the California Missions Trail
The John Muir Trail
The Pacific Crest Trail

SOUTH AMERICA

Aconcagua and the Southern Andes
Hiking and Biking Peru's Inca Trails
Trekking in Torres del Paine

AFRICA

Kilimanjaro
Walking in the Drakensberg
Walks and Scrambles in the Moroccan Anti-Atlas

NEW ZEALAND AND AUSTRALIA

Hiking the Overland Track

CHINA, JAPAN, AND ASIA

Annapurna
Hiking and Trekking in the Japan Alps and Mount Fuji
Hiking in Hong Kong
Japan's Kumano Kodo Pilgrimage
Japan's Kumano Kodo Pilgrimage
Trekking in Bhutan
Trekking in Ladakh
Trekking in Tajikistan
Trekking in the Himalaya

TECHNIQUES

Fastpacking
The Mountain Hut Book

MINI GUIDES

Alpine Flowers
Navigation
Pocket First Aid and Wilderness Medicine

MOUNTAIN LITERATURE

A Walk in the Clouds
Abode of the Gods
Fifty Years of Adventure
The Pennine Way — the Path, the People, the Journey
Unjustifiable Risk?

For full information on all our guides, books and eBooks, visit our website:
www.cicerone.co.uk